Learn HTML5 JavaScript for iOS

Scott Preston

Apress®

ISBN-13 (pbk): 978-1-4302-4038-9

ISBN-13 (electronic): 978-1-4302-4039-6

President and Publisher: Paul Manning
Lead Editor: Michelle Lowman
Developmental Editor: Gwenan Spearing, Matthew Moodie
Technical Reviewer: Peter Whitmore
Editorial Board: Steve Anglin, Ewan Buckingham, Gary Cornell, Louise Corrigan, Morgan Ertel, Jonathan Gennick, Jonathan Hassell, Robert Hutchinson, Michelle Lowman, James Markham, Matthew Moodie, Jeff Olson, Jeffrey Pepper, Douglas Pundick, Ben Renow-Clarke, Dominic Shakeshaft, Gwenan Spearing, Matt Wade, Tom Welsh
Coordinating Editor: Brent Dubi
Copy Editors: Valerie Greco, Jill Steinberg, James Compton, Kim Wimpsett
Compositor: Mary Sudul
Indexer: SPi Global
Cover Designer: Anna Ishchenko

Distributed to the book trade worldwide by Springer Science+Business Media New York, 233 Spring Street, 6th Floor, New York, NY 10013. Phone 1-800-SPRINGER, fax (201) 348-4505, e-mail orders-ny@springer-sbm.com, or visit www.springeronline.com.

For information on translations, please e-mail rights@apress.com, or visit www.apress.com.

Apress and friends of ED books may be purchased in bulk for academic, corporate, or promotional use. eBook versions and licenses are also available for most titles. For more information, reference our Special Bulk Sales–eBook Licensing web page at www.apress.com/bulk-sales.

Any source code or other supplementary materials referenced by the author in this text is available to readers at www.apress.com. For detailed information about how to locate your book's source code, go to www.apress.com/source-code.

This book is dedicated to my wife Emily & daughter Lilu.
Thanks for your patience, support and love.

Contents at a Glance

Contents

About the Author

 **Scott Preston** is a software craftsman from Columbus, Ohio. Over the past decade he has worked for some of the largest companies in the world and worked on lots of web and mobile sites. When he's not speaking at conferences, working on a new web or mobile project, or writing, he's busy solving hard problems for his customers at his company CodeGin LLC, which he founded in 2010. You can find out more about Scott on his blog http://www.scottpreston.com or follow him on twitter @scottpreston.

About the Technical Reviewer

Peter Whitmore is a software engineer with over fifteen years in the business. His experience has mostly been gained through his years with several manufacturing industry leaders. His development skills range from writing server side applications using Java to creating front end web applications written using frameworks and technologies such as spring, JSF, JSR 286 Portlets, dojo, jquery and standard JavaScript. Peter is also a registered Apple Developer for the iOS Developer Program.

Peter gained his Master of Science in software engineering at the University of Liverpool and currently manages a team of developers. He is married with two grown children and enjoys riding his bike, taking in the fresh air, listening to music, reading books and watching good dramas on television.

Preface

This book is designed to be used in conjunction with two sites. The first includes live working examples to accompany every chapter, and the second is a real world application that uses nearly every HTML5 or JavaScript feature discussed in the book, so you can see how it looks and works in practice.

The Companion Site

www.learnhtml5book.com

This site features a series of examples for every chapter. Look at the site on your desktop, iPad or iPhone as you read the book. Click "View Source" in your browser or go to the Apress download zip to see the source code for each example.

Whenever a companion site example is available, you will see a note that looks like this.

Companion Site Reference

Example 4-2: Follow the link below to run this example on the companion site.

http://www.learnhtml5book.com/chapter4/objects.php

You can navigate straight to the actual example on the companion site, view the source or "Save As" to see exactly what I'm talking about in real time.

If you have an eBook reader, you can click on the example link and go directly to the example on the companion site.

What you see in the book might only be part of the code needed to demonstrate an idea or concept, but the companion site has everything you need, like additional JS, or CSS, or rendered HTML. I also use a bit of PHP to glue together the HTML on the site, but you don't need to worry about that.

The Real World Example Site

www.grandviewave.com/m

The Grandview Avenue site was written in 2010 and continues to evolve. It's a real site designed to give local businesses an app and mobile site presence.

Each chapter in the book ends with a section called "Putting It All Together", in which I show you how I apply the concepts in the chapter to this real world application.

Hopefully you can see how this site works and either build one like it yourself, or do something completely different.

Downloading the code

The code for the examples shown in this book is available on the Apress web site, `www.apress.com`. A link can be found on the book's information page (`http://www.apress.com/9781430240389`) under the Source Code/Downloads tab. This tab is located underneath the Related Titles section of the page.

Contacting the Author

Should you have any questions or comments—or even spot a mistake you think we should know about—you can contact the author at `scott@learnhtml5book.com`.

CHAPTER 1

Getting Started

Congratulations! You are building your first web application for your iOS device (iPhone, iPad, or iPod Touch) using HTML5 and JavaScript.

You might think that you can pick up one of your HTML or JavaScript books from years past and then just scale it down to the size of your target device and you'll be good to go. You'd be wrong. A lot has changed.

In this chapter we lay the groundwork for building a mobile web app. Here we cover things like getting familiar with your browser, setting up your mobile project, architecting the site, and creating a site map as well as selecting the tools you'll use to build it.

All you need is an idea, and I'll help you take care of the rest.

You purchased this book to get started building a mobile web app. I won't beat around the bush and tell you about the history of the Internet or the history of browsers. Instead, let's just jump in.

Your Browser (Mobile Safari)

The browser we'll focus on is Mobile Safari—a WebKit-based browser engine that does an excellent job of parsing HTML5 and interpreting JavaScript.

■ **Note** Browsers use different rendering engines. Safari and Google Chrome use WebKit, Opera uses Presto, Firefox uses Gecko, and Internet Explorer uses Trident. In later chapters we'll need to use specific features of WebKit to achieve a more native-looking mobile web application.

Mobile Safari acts and renders in many ways similar to regular Safari, but it has a smaller screen, of course, and responds to gestures and touches as opposed to clicks. It also has noticeable performance differences and does not support Adobe Flash.

One of mobile Safari's most important screens is its Settings screen. You can get to it by clicking on Settings, and then Safari on the iPhone or iPad home screen. You'll see a screen like the one shown in Figure 1-1.

1

Figure 1-1. Safari Settings screen

Many of the settings here are straightforward and familiar to you from your desktop or laptop browser. Above all, I'd recommend that you set your **Advanced ➤ Debug Console** to On. This will help in debugging your app from within your simulator or on your phone. You can see this in Figure 1-2 below.

Figure 1-2. Debug settings for Safari

Planning Your Project

Before embarking on a mobile project, you need to have certain things in place, which I'll talk about next. If you're a seasoned web developer you probably know all of this stuff and can skip ahead; otherwise, keep in mind this is just an overview. If you have detailed questions, you can ask me via my site: http://www.learnhtml5book.com.

First, I'll talk about setting up your environment.

Local Environment

Fortunately, OS X comes with Apache built in. To enable Apache to work with your site, go to **System Preferences ➤ Sharing**, and then enable Apache by clicking on the Web Sharing box, as shown in Figure 1-3. You now have an Apache web server serving content from /Users/{username}/Sites.

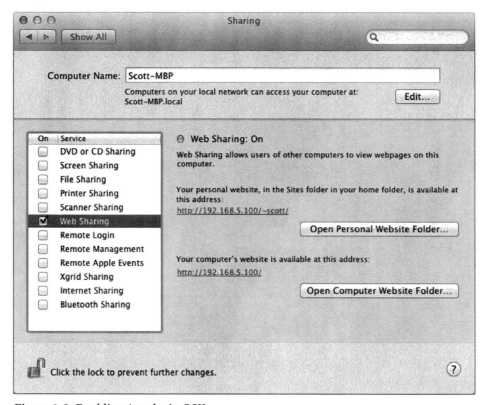

Figure 1-3. Enabling Apache in OSX

Remote Environment (Hosting)

If you don't have a web host for your site, you'll eventually need to get one. You have plenty to choose from. In the past I've had good luck with Host Gator (http://www.hostgator.com). You can get a site there starting at around $4 per month for Linux hosting.

Bug and Feature Tracking

Your site will not be perfect at launch, and you'll want to add features to it over time. For this, I'd recommend a ticketing and feature-tracking system.

If you want, you can start out with a spreadsheet or a text file, but for more elaborate projects you can use online sites like:

- http://16bugs.com

- http://www.lighthouseapp.com

Two other options, which even integrate with your version control system, are:

- Trac (http://trac.edgewall.org/)

- Redmine (http://www.redmine.org/)

Redmine is my current favorite.

Version Control

Every project needs version control software and there are two main version control systems out there. Basically, the two version control systems do the same thing—they keep track of your code:

- Subversion (SVN) keeps track of all your code in a single repository or server. SVN has been around a lot longer than Git (the other option), there's more documentation, and it's a little easier to learn and understand. You can find free online SVN providers including http://www.beanstalkapp.com and http://www.springloops.com.

- Git keeps track of everything locally and on a server. Git is newer and faster than SVN but is a little more difficult to understand. There are also free online providers like: http://www.github.com, and http://www.springloops.com.

If you don't know either, then pick Git; the investment is well worth it.

Deployments

At some point, you'll want to push your code to your host. You can do this in one of two ways:

- Manually, by uploading via FTP to your host

- Automatically, from your version control provider via online tools

Springloops (http://www.springloops.com) gives you the SVN or Git version control system, and then, based on schedule or commit, automatically deploys to your host. This will save you a lot of time and prevent you from overwriting files accidently.

Editor (IDE or Text Editor)

The editor is where you do *all* your work in building your site. You can choose to use either an IDE (integrated development environment) or a text editor.

- An IDE (like Xcode, Eclipse, Dreamweaver, PHPStorm, and RubyMine) has the added benefits of code/content assist, version control Integration, and color coding, all of which make your programming easier and you more productive.

- A text editor like TextMate, Vim, or Emacs can have the same features and there are extensions that allow some to come close to an IDE, but often the learning curve is a little steeper.

Site Integration

How do you want to integrate with your site? You can do this in one of two ways:

- Fully integrate: Everything all together in the same web project including the database code, your MVC framework, and your mobile site. The benefits of a fully integrated approach is you have less JavaScript and can build your pages on the fly.

- Service layer integration: You have your mobile site with HTML, CSS, and JavaScript, and all calls for data and interaction to your MVC framework are done via Ajax (asynchronous JavaScript and XML).

The benefits of the service layer integration is that you can add different mobile sites optimized for different browsers without changing your back end. You can also change your back end, for example from CakePHP to Ruby on Rails, and you won't need to change your mobile site at all. The last benefit is that turning your mobile site into a native app will be *very easy*.

I will use both these approaches for the sample mobile web app and native app. You will see the benefits of both methods as you progress through the building of your app.

Site Maps

There are two kinds of site maps:

- The first is what a web crawler like Google uses to better index a web site.

- The second is a high-level block diagram or outline of your site that shows all the pages and how they link together. That's the site map you need to create before you start your project.

You can create a sitemap either in a block diagram or with plain text. Sometimes block diagrams are better for explaining site structure to customers. A text version might look something like this:

- Home
- Page 1 (get data from web API)
    - Page 1 Detail 1 (get more data from web API)
    - Page 1 Detail 2
        - Detail 2 Info
- Page 2
- Contact
    - Link to Twitter
    - Link to Facebook
- About

Wireframes

A wireframe is a rough sketch of a page or screen without any colors or details. For this I recommend that you just take a blank iPhone or iPad template and start drawing what you want your app to look like.

Figure 1-4 shows a sample wireframe of a simple mobile web app with tabbed navigation at the bottom.

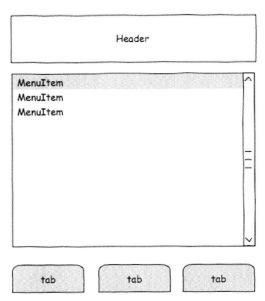

Figure 1-4. *Sample wireframe*

I created the above wireframe using a free Firefox plugin called Pencil.
You can find more about The Pencil Project here: http://pencil.evolus.vn.

Project Tracking and Management

Finally, to put everything together, especially if you're getting paid by someone to build this mobile web app, you need a project-tracking and management system. While this isn't a requirement for any of the programming in this book, it could aid you in communicating about the development of your application.

This can be as simple as using a spreadsheet or using a project management software product like Base Camp (http://basecamphq.com/).

The other tools I mentioned (Redmine, Trac, Springloops, and Lighthouse) also do a good job of tracking milestones, and some even come close to becoming full project management systems.

Application Components

Now you're almost ready to start building your mobile web app. But before we write any code, we need to put all the major parts of your application on the table to see how they fit together.

This will also form the large buckets for your project plan. This will help you estimate how long your project will take and at the same time give you a product launch checklist.

Your app will have several parts, each of which is detailed below and in Figure 1-5:

- **Site core** – The HTML pages of your web site

- **CSS** – The style sheets for your site that will determine it's look and feel

- **JavaScript** – The part of your site that allows it to interact with the APIs and to dynamically pull content from your site's database and API

- **External libraries** – The parts of your site like a mobile framework, jQuery, or plugins
- **Template components** –The parts of your site that are repeated over and over, like the header and footer and the navigation
- **External data** –The data your application will use—either on your server or stored locally on your iOS device
- **Phone data** –The data from your phone like your GPS or accelerometer data

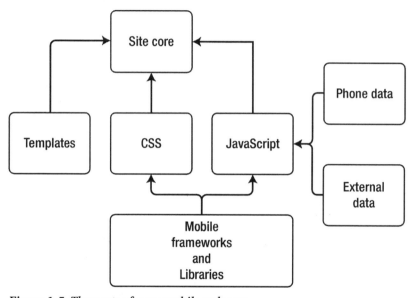

Figure 1-5. The parts of your mobile web app

Knowing these large buckets of your app beforehand will help you define and plan your project. Now we are ready to start coding.

Organizing Your Files

If you are working with a web project sometimes your files will be organized automatically for you via the web framework you've chosen. I've seen two methods for creating mobile sites:

- One is to give the mobile site its own subdomain like http://m.domain.com. This is the approach I took with the sample application in this book.
- The other is to have it run off a subdirectory like http://www.domain.com/mobile.

Subdomain (m.domain.com)

Using this structure allows you to create your own stand-alone mobile web application. The files do not need to mingle with the other files of your app.

Separating your code is important because your mobile web app might be using a different version of a JavaScript framework like jQuery, and having two versions of the same library on your site isn't a habit you want to start.

Subdirectory /m or /mobile

Sometimes you might want to reuse parts of your standard web site within your mobile site, or your mobile site is so simple that you don't need to create an entire web application and subdomain. If you have only a few pages in your mobile site or are experimenting with a few things, then just put your files in a subdirectory off the main web root.

Using a subdirectory is also more convenient if you want to create a mobile site for iPhone and iPad but share resources like images, CSS, and JavaScript frameworks from the main site.

Files to Organize

For a static web project there are really only four kinds of files to organize: cascading style sheets (CSS), JavaScript (JS), images (GIF, PNG, and JPG), and HTML.

To keep things organized I'd create a directory structure like this:

- **/** - for all HTML files

- **/css** - for all CSS

- **/js** - for all JavaScript

- **/images** - for all images Or, if your application structure is in a subdirectory:**/m** - for all HTML files

- **/m/css** - for all CSS

- **/m/js** - for all JavaScript

- **/m/images** - for all images.

How to link your files

You can use two mechanisms for linking files, relative and absolute linking.

- **Relative linking** uses a reference relative to the current file. For example if you have an image in **/images** or **/m/images** and your html is in either **/** or **/m**, you can create the following **<img>** tag to reference this file:

  ```
  <img src="images/someimage.jpg">
  ```

- **Absolute linking** creates two different links:

  ```
  <img src="/images/someimage.jpg">
  ```

  or

  ```
  <img src="/m/images/someimage.jpg">
  ```

From the above example you can see that **relative linking** is more flexible if you'll be refactoring the entire directory structure like all of the .html, .css and .js together, then you wouldn't need to make any changes since everything is relative. But **absolute linking** is easier to work with if your HTML files exist in multiple subdirectories.

For example, let's say you have four files:

- /index.html
- /subdir/index.html
- /subdir/subdir2/index.html
- /images/someimage.jpg

If you wanted image tags for the header and everything was relative, your <img> tags would look like this:

```
<img src="images/someimage.jpg">
<img src="../images/someimage.jpg">
<img src="../../images/someimage.jpg">
```

This is a mess if you want to use a common file for the header or navigation. It would be much easier to use:

```
<img src="/images/someimage.jpg">
```

for all three images.

What about multiple devices?

This directory structure might work for a single mobile web site, but eventually you may want to manage multiple devices like an iPhone and an iPad, and you will need a directory structure to facilitate that.

It's also a little complicated because you need to balance two things **code duplication** and **minimal regression testing**.

Let's say that you don't believe in having duplicate copies of code on your site. For example, you're using jQuery 1.4 and don't want to upgrade to a newer version because it's also used on your main web site and there's already a lot of code using it.

So you chug along and build your mobile web site only to find that the mobile framework you've chosen works best only with jQuery 1.6. What do you do?

- **Option A:** You live with two versions of jQuery on your site.

- **Option B:** You replace 1.4 with 1.6 and then retest everything to ensure that nothing broke.

- **Option C:** You replace 1.4 with 1.6 and don't retest because it shouldn't break anything.

Option A is the path we'll take for separate devices: an iPhone and an iPad. Option A has a directory structure that looks like this:

- /, /js, /css, /images – for all common assets
- /iphone, /iphone/css, /iphone/js, /iphone/images – for iPhone-only assets
- /ipad, /ipad/css, /ipad/js, /ipad/images – for iPad-only assets

This option allows for isolation and prevents large regression tests when working to enhance your site for a single device. The only thing it adds to the project is a few more files and, if they are needed, a few additional copies of libraries.

Now that we have a directory structure in mind, let's see how to make a change to your main web site's home page or root directory to point the mobile device to your new mobile web site.

Browser Redirection

When iPhone or iPad users come to your site, you don't want them to have to search for the mobile site button and you don't want to rely on them to know your mobile URL. To address this, you need to automatically send them there.

You can do this via Apache or JavaScript.

Companion Site Reference

Example 1-1: Follow the link below to run these examples on the companion site.

```
http://www.learnhtml5book.com/chapter1/redirect.php
```

Apache Redirection

Apache redirection first looks at the USER_AGENT sent in the HEADER of the request and then looks for a cookie if the user requests to be taken to the full site and not the mobile site. I've added the cookie because sometimes your mobile web site user might want to visit the normal, non-optimized site.

This method is preferred over JavaScript because it's done outside of code and you don't need to worry about overwriting or breaking it by mistake.

The example below redirects your user to the new domain m.domain.com, unless the nomobile cookie is set.

```
RewriteEngine On
RewriteCond %{HTTP_USER_AGENT} "iphone|ipod|ipad|googlebot-mobile" [NC]
RewriteCond %{HTTP_COOKIE} !^.*nomobile=true.*$
RewriteRule ^.*$ https://m.domain.com [R=301]
```

The next example redirects your user to the /m directory of your site, unless the nomobile cookie is set.

```
RewriteCond %{REQUEST_URI} !^/m/.*$
RewriteCond %{HTTP_USER_AGENT} "iphone|ipod|ipad|googlebot-mobile" [NC]
RewriteCond %{HTTP_COOKIE} !^.*nomobile=true.*$
RewriteRule ^(.*)$ /m/ [L,R=301]
```

JavaScript Redirection

If you don't have access to the Apache config, or mod_rewrite is not enabled on your server, you can use client-side redirection, as shown here. Just make sure to place this code in the <head> of your web page.

```
<script type="text/javascript">
    var isiPhone = navigator.userAgent.match(/iPhone/i);
    var isiPod = navigator.userAgent.match(/iPod/i);
    var isiPad = navigator.userAgent.match(/iPad/i);
    // check for mobile iOS device
    if(isiPhone || isiPod || isiPad) {
        if (!bypassRedirect()) {
            alert("redirecting user here");
            // window.location = '/m';
```

```
        } else {
            alert("user bypass message is true");
        }
    } else {
        alert("not a mobile device");
    }

    function bypassRedirect() {
        return false;
        // this logic will be added later in Chapter 12.
    }
</script>
```

Next, let's look at some vital tags that we'll use in our mobile app later in the chapter—and some that we won't use in this chapter, but that you may find useful in the future.

<meta>

Mobile Safari uses a few specific <meta> tags to optimize the mobile browser—things like viewport, scrolling, and whether or not to hide the address or status bar.

Here's a short description and the syntax.

apple-mobile-web-app-capable

Sets whether the web application runs in full-screen mode.

- Syntax:

  `<meta name="apple-mobile-web-app-capable" content="yes">`

- Description: When set to yes, the web application runs in full-screen mode outside of Safari. You also need to have saved this web app on the home screen of your iOS device.

apple-mobile-web-app-status-bar-style

Sets the style of the status bar if the web application is run in full screen mode.

- Syntax:

  `<meta name="apple-mobile-web-app-status-bar-style" content="black">`

- Description: Optional values are default, black, and black-translucent.

format-detection

Automatically detects the format of telephone numbers in a web page.

- Syntax

  `<meta name="format-detection" content="telephone=no">`

- Description: This is enabled by default; to disable this, set it to no.

viewport

The viewport is the area in a browser that contains the content of a web page; this area can be larger or smaller than the visible area. As it contains the contents of the web page, the size of the viewport affects how the contents are displayed and how text wraps. I'll show you how to work with the viewport in the next section.

The `viewport` meta tag sets the width and scale of the viewport. Normally, the iPhone will try to format the entire web site on the screen, and you have to zoom and scroll to read it on your mobile device. Using a combination of the values below, you can change how the site is rendered.

- Syntax
  ```
  <meta name="viewport" content="width=device-width">
  ```
- `width`: The width in pixels. The default is 980.
- `height`: The height in pixels. The default is calculated based on the width.
- `initial scale`: The default is calculated to fit the entire web page in the visible area.
- `minimum-scale`: The default is .25.
- `maximum-scale`: The default is 1.6.
- `user-scalable`: Determines whether a user can zoom in and out.
- `device-width` & `device-height`: The width and height of the device in pixels.

Screen Size and Viewport

One thing you'll note about the different screen sizes and viewports of the iPhone, iPhone4, and iPad is the DPI. While your iPhone4 with retina display has a higher resolution and DPI, your web site is still best viewed at 320×480. The iPad is optimized for the same working area as an older laptop or PC. I'll talk more about scaling for the retina display in Chapter 3.

While you might think you have the entire pixel size to work with, you really don't because the address, status, and button bars take up substantial room. In portrait orientation on an iPhone, the address and status bars take up 80 pixels at the top, and the button bar takes up 44 pixels at the bottom, so the working area is smaller than the actual screen, as summarized in Table 1-1.

Table 1-1. Example Screen Size Matrix

Device	Resolution	DPI	Working Area
iPhone	320×480 (portrait)	163dpi	320×356
iPhone4	640×960 (portrait)	326dpi	640×712
iPad	1024×768 (landscape)	132dpi	1024×674

The various bars take up slightly less room in landscape orientation, so here's an example of an iPhone turned on its side. The actual pixels you have to work with are 480×208. That's 80 pixels for the address and status bars and 32 pixels for the button bar, as shown in Figure 1-6.

Figure 1-6. *Landscape screen real estate*

Let's see how this affects a mobile web page: When viewing a web site on the iPhone in full screen mode (no <meta> viewport is set), you get a screen like the one shown in Figure 1-7.

Companion Site Reference

Example 1-2: Follow the link below to run this example on the companion site.

http://www.learnhtml5book.com/chapter1/fullscreen.php

Figure 1-7. *Full screen example (no viewport tag used)*

The iPhone has a default viewport of 980 pixels. So if the site you are viewing is larger than that, it will zoom out to fit, as is the case in Figure 1-7. If the site you are viewing is optimized for a smaller width, then you might need to zoom in to read the site.

This means that a 320-pixel iPhone showing 980 pixels of space has a zoom level of .3.

All of this kind of calculation can give you a headache. Fortunately, there's a way around this, and that's to specify the viewport the device should use.

Because we want to build a site optimized for mobile browsers, we'll add the following meta tag and change how the page is viewed and zoomed, with the results shown in Figure 1-8.

```
<meta name="viewport" content="width=device-width" />
```

Companion Site Reference

Example 1-3: Follow the link below to run this example on the companion site.

`http://www.learnhtml5book.com/chapter1/viewport.php`

Figure 1-8. Same page with viewport <meta> tag

This takes care of auto-sizing your web site. All you need to do now is make sure your images and styles support this height and width.

The Sample App

This book follows the process of creating a mobile web site and iPhone app for www.grandviewave.com (Grandview Avenue dot com). At the end of each chapter I'll have a *Putting It All Together* section where I'll discuss my sample app and how to use the knowledge in that chapter to enhance and modify a real-world application.

Grandview is a small community a few miles from downtown Columbus and The Ohio State University. It has a main drag called Grandview Avenue on which there are 50-plus businesses ranging from dance studios and movie theaters to coffee shops and bars.

Living just a few blocks away I always wanted to have a way to contact a local restaurant for reservations, or I'd want to know what band was playing at Grandview Café that evening. But none of the social apps seemed to have the data all in one place or with sufficient detail to get this information. So I created www.grandviewave.com and a simple iPhone app called Grandview Ave.

Figure 1-9. The web version of grandviewave.com

I also need to mention that I had a lot of help on the project from a local business on Grandview Avenue called Iannarino Dexter Creative. Joe helped me spread the word about the site and app, Mike helped with the logo design, and Kate helped design the site.

Until this year the site was rather basic and just listed names of businesses and had a few features like Near Me using GPS. But upon deciding to write this book, I thought why not enhance Grandview Ave and at the same time provide an app and framework for others to use to build their own community sites. You can see the web version in Figure 1-9.

You can see from the web site it's rather simple. It has a business directory, events, news, and specials as well as information about the site and parking. Throughout this book we are going to enhance this site and reinvent the mobile experience. In fact, we're going to start from scratch completely. Table 1-2 shows the various tools I used when creating the mobile web app.

Table 1-2. Project Checklist

Project Item	Sample App Solution
Hosting	Local and VPS (virtual private server)
Bug and feature tracking	Redmine
Version control	Subversion (SVN)
Deployments	Custom scripts
Editor	Textmate and PHPStorm
Data and site integration	Service calls via Ajax & JSON
Sitemap	To be done later
Wireframes	To be done later
Project tracking	Spreadsheet

Because we're starting from scratch, the first development version of the mobile app you'll see will be very plain (see Figure 1-10). It will have a filler image, followed by normal-looking HTML with a default font.

The only thing applied will be the <meta> viewport discussed earlier in this chapter. It will have no HTML5, JavaScript, CSS, or anything resembling an iPhone app. Hopefully, this is exactly what you are starting with since you're learning how to build an app from scratch.

Figure 1-10. Skeleton of new site for http://www.grandviewave.com/m

This site will have the directory structure shown in Figure 1-11.

Figure 1-11. Directory structure of m.grandviewave.com

Since we are going to build the app as we go, this content will gradually change and might grow rather large, so you won't see some of the code from the previous sections described too much. I'll include the <meta> information below, but you might not see that same header markup in later chapters.

Companion Site Reference

Example 1-4: Follow the link below to run this example on the companion site.

`http://www.learnhtml5book.com/chapter1/samplehome.php`

```html
<html>
<head>
    <title>Sample Header?</title>
    <meta name="viewport" content="width=device-width" />
</head>
<body>
<h1>Sample Header?</h1>
<hr><div><img src="sample_300.png"/></div>
<p>Navigation?</p>
<ul>
    <li>Businesses</li>
    <li>Near Me</li>
    <li>Sales &amp; Specials</li>
    <li>Parking</li>
    <li>The Avenue Hunt</li>
    <li>Audio &amp; Video</li>
    <li>About</li>
    <li>Contact</li>
</ul>
</body>
<html>
```

Now if you look at this page it's like you'd expect: just regular HTML. I recommend you open up your favorite editor and create a simple page that you want to be the base for your new mobile web app.

Summary

The main thing I want you to take away from this chapter is knowing where to start and creating a very simple viewported web site using nothing more than an extra <meta> tag and simple HTML.

To save you some time later on, I showed you a few ways to set up your project and organize your files.

Finally, I talked a little bit about a sample application we are going to build through the chapters in this book.

Before moving on to the next chapter, you should know how to do the following:

- Configure Mobile Safari for development.

- Create a plan for your mobile web app, including a local environment & version control.

- Know if you're going to use a subdomain or subdirectory.

- Know how to redirect a user from the main site to your mobile site.

- Know how to use the <meta> tags to create a viewport for your iOS device.

I also introduced you to the sample app I'm going to create throughout this book.

Next I'll give a short overview of HTML5—mainly the parts you'll want to use to start building your own web app.

CHAPTER 2

HTML5 in Short

This chapter is not a complete reference on HTML5, but it teaches you enough about HTML5 to be dangerous.

This chapter also does not go into detail on some of the most popular elements of HTML5 such as <canvas>, <audio>, and <video>. Those elements require an entire chapter of discussion, which will come later in this book.

Instead, this chapter provides an overview of some HTML5-based APIs including web workers, web sockets, and geolocation.

So what do I talk about in this chapter? Mainly three things:

- What HTML5 is and isn't

- The new HTML5 structural elements and attributes

- The new HTML5 form input types and attributes

Then I show you how I applied those new features to my sample app, Grandview Avenue, to show you how you would use some of these HTML5 features in a real-world application. Figure 2-1 shows the official logo of HTML5.

Figure 2-1. Official HTML5 Logo

What Is HTML5?

First and foremost HTML5 is still in DRAFT state. That means that nothing I tell you today is 100% guaranteed to be in the official specification when it's released. That being said, all of the current browsers, Internet Explorer, Firefox, Chrome, Safari, and Opera, are all racing as fast as they can to get as much of the HTML5 "DRAFT" in their desktop and mobile browsers.

If you ask someone about HTML5 you'll either hear something about the official specification by the W3C or you'll hear about some of the features that are new and cool but not yet finalized, such as web workers.

I talk about all of the new cool stuff and am not completely strict on what's in the HTML5 specification. But ironically I think the best way to tell you about HTML5 is to start by telling you what it's *not*.

It's Not XHTML

This means that it does not need to follow XML validation as the following statements are equivalent.

```
1:<div id=container>This is a div<br></div>
```

and

```
2:<div id="container">This is another div<br/></div>
```

So although clearly statement 1 would not pass an XML/XHTML validation, HTML5 ensures that both of these statements are rendered in exactly the same way.

It's Not HTML4 +1

You have to admit the previous versions of HTML and XHTML were a little lofty in their goals. The idea was a standards body would create a specification for how to mark up a page and all the browser vendors would follow this standard 100% and we'd all be living in the land of unicorns and rainbows right? Wrong!

What happened was that you'd end up with one browser that would implement some subset of the specification, and create its own stuff. Then you'd get another browser to implement a different subset of the specification and add its own stuff, which basically vetoed the W3C's specification.

HTML5 needed to start and work differently. So what happened? Basically they started the other way around. They went to each of the major browser vendors, Microsoft, Mozilla, Google, Apple, and Opera and asked, "What do you want in the specification? What can you all agree on?" They ended up with:

- A set of tags

- A set of attributes

- A set of new form input types and form attributes

- A set of new APIs

So now you could still have the browser vendors going out doing their own thing, but if they didn't agree on the tags/attributes/APIs it would not go into the specification. That meant that the specification was now supported by everyone.

HTML5 Is Not Just Markup

HTML5 is not just tags but it's also a set of JavaScript APIs to provide a richer user experience. The APIs also tried to enhance the core foundations of the browser APIs. So rather than having to use a JavaScript framework for selector features, the document now has selectors. Now rather than having to access native custom written APIs for geolocation, the document has functions such as getCurrentPosition.

Here's a short summary of the new API features you will have with your new HTML5 document.

Selectors

This is document.getElementById on steroids, or all the goodness of jQuery at your fingertips in native JavaScript. By expanding the criteria in which you can select a document element, you make it much easier to access the elements in your page either individually or grouped.

```
<script type="text/javascript">
var elts1 = document.getElementsByClassName("someclass");
var elts2 = document.querySelectorAll("ul li:first-child");
var elt1 = document.querySelector("#someid");
</script>
```

Canvas and Drawing

This gives you the ability to draw in the page. I talk more about this element in Chapter 9. This example draws a red square.

Companion Site Reference

Example 2-1: Follow the link below to run this example on the companion site.

```
http://www.learnhtml5book.com/chapter2/canvas.php
```

```
<canvas id="simplecanvas"></canvas>
<script type="text/javascript">
var canvas = document.querySelector('#simplecanvas');
var ctx = canvas.getContext('2d');
ctx.fillStyle='rgb(255,0,0)';
ctx.fillRect(0,0,100,100);
</script>
```

Media Playback

This gives you greater control over the audio and video playback. I talk more about this in Chapter 10. This example loads a test video and plays it within the video tag.

Companion Site Reference

Example 2-2: Follow the link below to run this example on the companion site.

`http://www.learnhtml5book.com/chapter2/video.php`

```
<video width="400" height="225" controls="controls" id="myvid">
<source src="grandviewave-test.m4v" type="video/mp4;" >
</video>
<script type="text/javascript">
var v = document.querySelector('#myvid');
v.play();
</script>
```

Offline Storage

This does not have a JavaScript component, but it allows images or other assets to be stored offline, for example, by adding this to the <html> tag:

`<html manifest="/cache.manifest">`

your browser receives a manifest file which looks like:

```
CACHE MANIFEST
/css/grandview.css
/js/grandview.js
/images/grandview.png
```

allowing these files to be retrieved locally in the event that you're offline. I talk more about this feature in Chapter 12.

Local and Session Storage

Local and session storage allows you to store items in your web browser as Name–Value pairs versus an SQL database as in Web SQL Storage. You can think of this as a really powerful client-side cookie.

Local storage stores data forever until you delete it. *Session* stores it for one session. Both have methods for setItem and removeItem allowing you to store and retrieve. I talk more about this in Chapter 12.

Document Editing

Editing elements is now very easy and you do this by just specifying the attribute:

`contenteditable="true"`

This allows a particular part of the page to be editable but by itself it's rather limited, so to make use of it you need to access the element's edited content.

Companion Site Reference

Example 2-3: Follow the link below to run this example on the companion site.

http://www.learnhtml5book.com/chapter2/edits.php

So if you're editing the following markup, all you need to do is click on the content section, then the "Save" button.

```
<div id="test" contenteditable="true">This is some silly text.</div>
<button onclick="save()">Save</button>
<script type="text/javascript">
function save() {
var content = document.querySelector("#test").innerHTML;
alert(content); // or do something else
}
</script>
```

Document Messaging

Prior to HTML5, web browsers prevented sites from accessing each other if they had different origins or were on different domains (aka "Cross-Site Scripting"). This was a preventive security measure.

This means that one part of the document that lived on www.domain1.com could not talk to a document that lived on www.domain2.com. The cross-document messaging API in HTML5 allows this while also providing security. I talk more about document messaging in Chapter 14.

Web Sockets

Web sockets are amazing. They eliminate the need for polling so that if, for example, you have some data that are changed on the server, instead of polling the server every few seconds or minutes to look for an update, your server can send a message to the client with the update (note: link only for example purposes):

```
var ws = new WebSocket("ws://m.grandviewave.com/test");
ws.send("anything new?");
```

Web sockets will allow your mobile web application and your server to communicate in real time. I talk more about this in Chapter 14.

Drag and Drop

HTML5 provides the ability to drag and drop elements by adding two attributes, draggable and dropzone. Unfortunately it's not supported by Mobile Safari. My guess is that it was difficult to get this to work with a multitouch interface and it works best with a mouse and buttons.

History Management

Prior to HTML5 the best way to know your history in a rich (Ajax-based) web page was to poll the location.hash property on a timer.

HTML5 now provides an API that allows you to access the location.hash and in fact gives you a more robust mechanism for accessing the entire history of a session.

The event fires when the hash has changed as onHashChange. The methods added to the history object are pushDate() and replaceState() allowing you to put items into and retrieve items from the history object. I talk more about this in Chapter 14.

Microdata

Microdata are used to give semantic meaning to a web page. For example, how's the web or a system supposed to know that the text on a page is an "Event" that takes place at a specific time and place? Well it can't, unless you parse through and look for data and times and geolocation data. But then what might work for one website won't work for another because the HTML would be in a different format.

Microdata add the following attributes to provide this kind of semantic meaning to the content on a page: itemscope, itemtype, itemid, itemprop, and itemref. Unfortunately Microdata are not supported in Safari Mobile at this time.

Geolocation

Geolocation is the ability of your mobile browser to identify its position using a GPS (global positioning system). The mechanism is basically defined by the following example.

```
navigator.geolocation.getCurrentPosition(successFunction, errorFunction);

function successFunction(pos) {
        // do something here with pos
}

function errorFunction(err) {
        // do something with the error
}
```

I talk extensively about geolocation and interaction with Google Maps in Chapter 7.

File API

HTML5 now provides a mechanism for working with local files. Specifically the specification talks about the following kinds of local files.

- FileList: This is an array of files in the local system.
- Blob: This represents raw binary data.
- File: This is read-only and is a collection of information attributes such as name and date of last modification.
- FileReader: Provides methods to read a File or Blob.
- FileError: Provides for error conditions that occur when using the File API.

Unfortunately Mobile Safari does not support the File API at this time.

Web Workers

Web workers are used for JavaScript-based threading and running JavaScript in the background. The worker interface has two methods, `terminate()` and `postMessage()`. Let's say I wanted to load some data in the background; I might create a worker like this:

```
<script type="text/javascript">
var dataWorker = new Worker('data.js');
dataworker.onmessage = function(event) {
        // enable navigation
};
</script>
```

I talk more about web workers in Chapter 14.

HTML5 Support

If you plan on using HTML5 for all mobile browsers, know that all browsers don't support HTML5 in the same way as Mobile Safari. Mobile Safari on the iPhone, iPod Touch, and iPad don't completely support everything that's in HTML5 either. Table 2-1 gives a summary. Although they grade out at over 90% you might want to keep some of these things in mind when designing your mobile web app.

Table 2-1. HTML5 Features with Limited or No Support in Mobile Safari

Limited / No Support	Description
Audio and Video Codecs	No support for Ogg, WebM
Text Markup	Missing support for certain elements at this time
Form Attributes	Missing support for certain input types and related tags
Drag and Drop	Touch interface not conducive to Drag/drop interactions built for mouse
Microdata	No support at this time
3D Canvas	Battery and resource constraints
Files API	No support at this time
Webcam	No support at this time
Web Notifications	No support at this time

For a complete list of how much HTML5 support you have in your browser, go to HTML5 Test (`http://html5test.com`), where it will tell you how much of HTML5 tags and APIs are supported.

You can also stay tuned for later versions of iOS as support for many of these features will be available.

HTML5 Overview

This is a quick-reference guide to how to use HTML5 for your mobile website.

DOCTYPE and UTF-8

To use HTML5 all you need are the following three lines.

```
<!doctype html>
<html>
<meta charset="utf-8">
```

Because you can also use `<meta charset=utf-8 />` or even `<meta CHARSET='utf-8'>`, your programming style is important for readability and maintainability. So pick a style and stick with it.

New Attributes

These are some new global attributes added to HTML5; you can add these attributes to any element.

- `Contenteditable ="true|false"`: Allows you to a make an element editable.
- `contextmenu="menu_id"`: Associates the element with a menu element.
- `draggable="true|false|auto"`: Specifies whether you can drag an element.
- `dropzone="copy|move|link"`: Specifies what happens when an item is dragged on this element.
- `Hidden`: Hides an element.
- `spellcheck="true|false"`: Specifies whether an element needs its spelling or grammar checked.

New Structural Tags

All of these new tags are designed to give more semantic meaning and replace all of the custom CSS classNames and IDs given to `<div>` tags.

<article>

This is like a `<div>` or `<section>` element but can be used for content like a blog entry or in a forum post to give more semantic meaning.

```
<article>
        <h1>This is an article.</h1>
        <p>Article Content...</p>
</article>
```

<aside>

This is content that is aside from the content in which it's placed. It should be related to the surrounding content.

```
<aside>
        <p>This is content aside from the main part.</p>
</aside>
```

<details>

This is used to describe the parts or details of a document (not currently supported by Mobile Safari).

```
<details>
        <p>All rights reserved.</p>
</details>
```

<figure> and <figcaption>

This is an image within a document and its caption.

```
<figure>
        <figcaption>This is a nice picture!</figcaption>
        <img src="nice.jpg">
</figure>
```

<footer>

This is the footer of a document.

```
<footer>
        Footer of page.
</footer>
```

<header>

And this is the header of a document.

```
<header>
        Header of page
</header>
```

<hgroup>

This is a section of headings grouped together: <h1>, <h2>, and so on.

```
<hgroup>
        <h1>Heading1</h1>
        <h2>Heading2</h2>
</hgroup>
```

<mark>

This is text that should be highlighted.

```
<p>The quick brown <mark>fox</mark> jumped over the lazy dog.</p>
```

\<nav\>

This is the navigation section of a document.

```
<nav>
        Site navigation
</nav>
```

\<progress\>

This is an indicator of work in progress (not supported by Mobile Safari).

```
<progress value="2" max="5">
</progress>
```

\<ruby\>

These are Chinese notes or characters (limited support).

\<rp\>

This is what to show browsers instead of the \<ruby\> element.

\<rt\>

This is used for explanation of the ruby element.

\<section\>

This is a section of a document such as \<header\> or \<footer\> but more generic.

```
<section>
        <h1>This is a section.</h1>
        <p>Section Content...</p>
</section>
```

\<time\>

This is used for defining a time or date (not supported).

```
<p>Hours of operation are from: <time>10AM<time> to <time>10PM</time>.</p>
```

\<wbr\>

This is used for defining a good place for a word break.

```
<p>The name of the book web site is http://www.<wbr>learnhtml5book<wbr>.com.</p>
```

Figure 2-2 shows a simple page built from some of these new structural elements. I've used the following bit of CSS to highlight the different elements.

```
<style>
header,nav,footer,article,section {margin:5px;}
header,nav,footer {border:1px solid #000;}
section {border:1px dotted green;}
</style>
```

Companion Site Reference

Example 2-4: Follow the link below to run this example on the companion site.

`http://www.learnhtml5book.com/chapter2/structure.php`

Figure 2-2. *New Elements with Simple CSS*

New Media Tags

Audio and video, along with <source> and <embed>, get their own chapter later in the book (Chapter 10), so I don't say much about them here. I just quickly summarize the files and attributes they support.

\<audio> and \<video>

The \<audio> tags support .wav, .mp3, and .acc files, and the attributes autoplay, controls, loop, preload, and src. iOS supports only MPEG4 and H.264 video codecs, but it supports all these attributes: audio, autoplay, controls, height, width, loop, poster, preload, and src.

\<source>

Used in conjunction with either the \<audio> or \<video> tags, this child element helps to define the source of the media. It has the attributes media, src, and type.

\<embed>

This tag defines embedded content such as a .swf file. It has the attributes height, src, type, and width.

New Form Tags

Here's a list of some of the new form tags available to you in HTML5.

\<datalist>

The datalist element defines a list of options. You can think of this as a predefined auto-complete (not supported).

```
<datalist id="categories">
<option value="Restaurant">
<option value="Personal Services">
<option value="Night Life">
</datalist>
```

\<fieldset>

This defines a logically grouped set of field elements (limited support).

```
<form>
<fieldset>
<legend>Form:</legend>
    Name: <input type="text">
    Email: <input type="text">
</fieldset>
</form>
```

\<keygen>

This generates a public–private key pair.

```
Encryption: <keygen name="securityKey" />
```

\<meter>

This defines a measurement within a known range (not supported).

```
<meter value="5" min="0" max="10">5 of 10</meter>
```

<output>

This represents the result of a calculation.

New Form Input Types

There is a whole range of new input types provided by HTML5.

type='tel'

This allows for the input of a phone number. On the iPhone it will also display a phone dial pad for input.

```
Tel: <input type="tel" required="required">
```

type='search'

This is used for search fields such as Google or site search.

```
Search: <input type="search" required="required">
```

type='url'

This is used for fields that should contain a URL address.

```
URL: <input type="url" required="required">
```

type='email'

This is used for fields that should contain an email address.

```
Email: <input type="email" required="required">
```

type='datetime'

This is used for fields that should contain a date and time.

```
DateTime: <input type="datetime" required="required">
```

type='date'

This is used for fields that should contain a date. What's really nice is that in some of these fields Mobile Safari will provide you automatic date select widgets, as you can see in Figure 2-3.

```
Date: <input type="date" required="required">
```

Figure 2-3. *Example of Date Input Type*

type='month'

This is used for fields that should contain a month.

```
Month: <input type="month" required="required">
```

type='week'

This is used for fields that should contain a week (no customized user-interface).

```
Week: <input type="week" required="required">
```

type='time'

This is used for fields that should contain a time.

```
Time: <input type="time" required="required">
```

type='datetime-local'

This is used for fields that should contain a time in the local time zone of the user.

```
DateTime: <input type="datetime-local" required="required">
```

type='range'

This is a slider used for fields that are within a numerical range.

```
Range: <input type="range" required="required">
```

type='color'

This is used for fields that should contain a color.

```
Color: <input type="color" required="required">
```

When you put all these form elements together you get the following sample page. Most of these fields look like <input type="text">, however, from Figure 2-3 you can see that there's sometimes a custom user-interface designed to allow for easier input.

Sample Form Code

Here's an example of a form using the new input types. This form will prompt you for valid inputs (such as a valid URL), but doesn't do anything with the data.

Companion Site Reference

Example 2-5: Follow the link below to run this example on the companion site.

```
http://www.learnhtml5book.com/chapter2/form.php
```

```
<form id="test" action="form.php" >
Number: <input type="number" name="number" placeholder="Enter a number"↵
  autofocus="autofocus" required><br>
Email: <input type="email" required="required" placeholder="Enter an email"><br>
URL: <input type="url" required="required"><br>
Date: <input type="date" required="required"><br>
Week: <input type="week" required="required"><br>
Month: <input type="month" required="required"><br>
DateTime: <input type="datetime" required="required"><br>
Time: <input type="time" required="required"><br>
Range: <input type="range" required="required"><br>
Search: <input type="search" required="required"><br>
Tel: <input type="tel" required="required"><br>
<input type="submit">
</form>
```

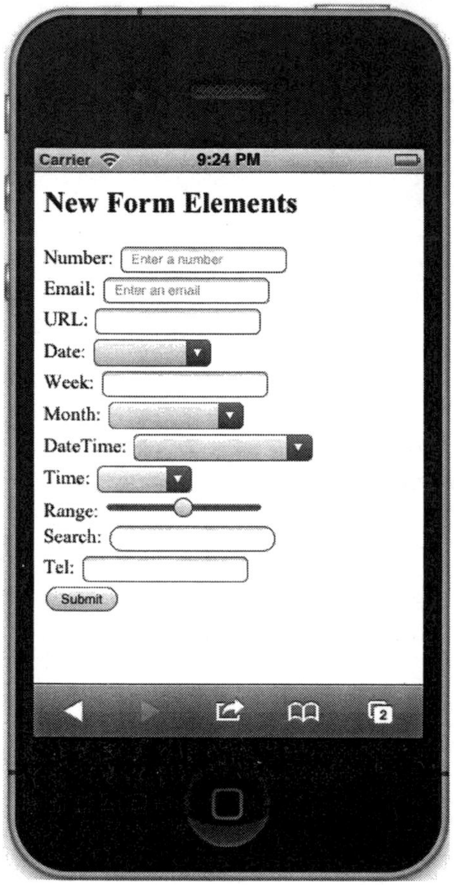

Figure 2-4. All form elements

Additional Form Element Attributes

HTML5 provides some useful additional attributes for the input types in your forms (see Figure 2-4). For example, this is the markup for an email input type with autofocus and placeholder text:

```
Email: <input type="email" required="required" placeholder="Enter your email"↵
autofocus required>
```

These new attributes assist in form behavior and form validation.

- autocomplete: Specifies that the field should have an autocomplete function
- autofocus: Specifies that the field should be focused on
- loadform: Specifies one or more forms to which the field belongs
- formaction: An override for the action property of the elements form

- `formenctype`: An override for the type property of the elements form
- `formmethod`: An override for the method of the elements form
- `formnovalidate`: An override of the elements form telling it not to validate
- `formtarget`: An override from the elements form specifying a different target
- `height` and `width`: Used in conjunction with the image input type, specifying its height and width
- `list`: Used in conjunction with the datalist field, specifying the ID of the datalist
- `min`, `max`, and `step`: These are used to specify restrictions to the input types containing numbers or dates
- `multiple`: Like the select tag, other input types such as input type=file can now contain multiple values so that multiple files can be uploaded
- `novalidate`: Tells the form not to validate on submission
- `pattern`: A regular expression pattern to be used when validating a particular input type
- `placeholder`: Placeholder text instead of a blank field
- `required`: Tells the form that the current element is required and must be validated prior to submission

Removed Tags

I wrap up this quick reference to HTML5 with a list of some of the tags that have been removed from the HTML specification. To be honest, some of them are tags I've never even used!

- `<acronym>`
- `<applet>`
- `<basefont>`
- `<big>`
- `<center>`
- `<dir>`
- `<font>`
- `<frame>`
- `<frameset>`
- `<noframes>`
- `<strike>`
- `<tt>`
- `<u>`
- `<xmp>`

Choosing HTML5 Features to Use in Your Apps

The main thing to remember about HTML5 is that it's still a draft. Although most of the elements and APIs surrounding the HTML5 specification are still under review, a vast majority of everything you see today will be there when it becomes official.

Because browser vendors have the ultimate veto power of what gets in the spec, I would look to future browser releases and their support of certain HTML5 features as a means of determining whether you should implement that particular part of the spec.

Putting It All Together

This chapter just focused on structural and form elements, and so that's what I created in the sample app to show you how you might use some of these elements in a real-world project.

I left the sample app with a standard viewport HTML page, but there was no DOCTYPE, or HTML5-based structural elements. The header was:

```
<html>
<head>
<title>Sample Header?</title>
<meta name="viewport" content="width=device-width" />
</head>
<body>
```

But now with our new HTML5 tags, that page looks a little different.

```
<!doctype html>
<html>
<head>
<title>Sample Header?</title>
<meta charset="utf-8">
<meta name="viewport" content="width=device-width" />
</head>
<body>
```

This now tells our browser to start rendering the page with HTML5 specific tags. This header appears in the source code for every example in the book, so I just assume you've got it and I won't repeat it each time I start a new example.

Adding the New Structural Elements to the Homepage

The only part of the HTML5 spec I currently use in the sample app is the new structural elements; specifically, I use these new elements in my mobile app:

- `<header>`: For the header of the app.
- `<nav>`: For the site navigation. I think I'll use two kinds of navigation, in-page list navigation and tabbed navigation (discussed in Chapter 6).
- `<footer>`: For the site footer.
- `<section>`: For the sections of the page.
- `<figure>` and `<figcaption>`: I use these for the photos on the site of the businesses or of the events.

Here is the markup for my sample home page so far, including these new elements.

```
<!doctype html>
<html>
<head>
<title>Sample Header?</title>
<meta charset="utf-8">
<meta name="viewport" content="width=device-width" />
<link rel="stylesheet" href="css/chapter2.css" type="text/css" />
</head>
<body>
<header>
<h1>Sample Header?</h1>
</header>
<section>
<div><img src="media/sample_300.png"/></div>
</section>
<nav>
<p>Navigation?</p>
<ul>
<li>Businesses</li>
<li>Near Me</li>
<li>Sales &amp; Specials</li>
<li>Parking</li>
<li>The Avenue Hunt</li>
<li>Audio &amp; Video</li>
<li>About</li>
<li>Contact</li>
</ul>
</nav>
<footer>
Nothing Yet
</footer>
</body>
<html>
```

So although not that impressive, it gives us the hooks we need for styling in the next chapter and functionality throughout the rest of the book.

Next I want to have a way to capture email addresses on the new app. So for that I use the email type and I also want to perform some basic validation.

A Sample Contact Form with Validation

The form uses just the email type, but I also use required and placeholder attributes. I could do more with the form upon validation, but for now I just want to print an alert on the page.

```
<form id="test" action="stay.php" >
Email: <input type="email" required placeholder="Enter an email"><br>
<input type="submit">
</form>
<script type="text/javascript">
    var f  = document.querySelector("form");
        f.onsubmit = function() {
```

```
        if (f.checkValidity()) {
            alert("form ok");
        } else {
            alert("form not ok");
        }
    };
</script>
```

Chapter Summary

This chapter talked about three major areas of HTML5:

- *API Overview*: These are the new JavaScript APIs available to you including Geolocation, web workers, web sockets, and so on.

- *Structural Elements*: Items intended to replace CSS IDs and ClassNames, such as <header>, <footer>, <section>, and so on.

- *Form Input Type Attributes*: These are extensions of the <input> tag to include a broader form datatype including date, email, range, and so on.

There are other parts of HTML5 that I only mentioned briefly because I go over those in greater detail in later chapters. They include:

- Geolocation (Chapter 7)

- Canvas (Chapter 9)

- Audio and video (Chapter 10)

- Offline apps and local storage (Chapter 12)

- Web workers and web sockets (Chapter 14)

I also updated the sample app to include the basic HTML5 structural elements, started to sketch out the home page, and added a form with basic form processing.

Before moving on to the next chapter you should know how to do the following.

- Know how make your document an HTML5 document with the DOCTYPE.

- Be able to create and use HTML5 structural elements and attributes.

- Be able to create and use HTML5 form input types and attributes.

- Know enough about the API components to start thinking of how you want to use these features in your mobile web app.

Next, I discuss how to make your app look like a native iPhone app.

CHAPTER 3

CSS3 and iOS Styling

If you want your mobile site to look like a native app you'll need to spend some time learning the new features of CSS3. In particular there are new features that allow your lists to take on a native look and feel and new features to create awesome buttons as well as novel ways to use backgrounds or create stunning effects.

One way to create these effects is with query selectors and learning how to optimize your CSS for Retina Displays or optimizing for orientation. You might even want to be able to save your web application to the home screen of your iPad or iPhone.

Because CSS3 is a lot different than CSS1 or CSS2 I spend a little bit of time telling you about the differences. This will allow you to navigate the documentation and specification on the web to find exactly what you need if you don't find it here.

What is CSS3?

First and foremost CSS stands for cascading stylesheets.

CSS Level 1 (or CSS1) was first published in December of 1996. This version of the CSS is no longer maintained.

CSS Level 2 (or CSS2) was first published in 1998 and is a superset of CSS1; it added features including positioning and z-index. Again this version of the CSS is no longer maintained.

CSS Level 2 revision 1 (or CSS2.1) was first published in 2005. It was only published as a recommendation on June 7th, 2011.

CSS Level 3 (or CSS3) is a little different. It uses CSS2.1 as its core and builds upon this core module by module rather than an entire set of specifications.

For a complete list of CSS modules you can visit the W3C here:

`http://www.w3.org/Style/CSS/current-work`

We are talking about only the following modules for this book.

- Media Queries
- Backgrounds and Borders
- Font
- 2D/3D Transformations
- Transitions and Animations
- Text Effects
- Overflow

CSS Basics

Before we talk about anything new there are a few fundamentals we need to take care of, such as how to place CSS on your site and how to select specific styles for specific devices (iPhone or iPad).

Using Your CSS

Question: Do you embed your CSS in your page or externalize it (put it in a separate .css file)?

Answer: Sometimes for testing I put the CSS in my page where I can have visibility to all the rules and properties, but this generally isn't a good idea because it makes CSS rules less reusable and more difficult to maintain. Inline CSS looks like this:

```
<head>
<style>
header,nav,footer,article,section {margin:5px;}
header,nav,footer {border:1px solid #000;}
section {border:1px dotted green;}
</style>
</head>
```

When you want to externalize your CSS there are two ways: one is to link your document via the `<link>` tag, and the second is to import your document via the @import rule.

\<link\>

As a good practice you externalize your CSS via a `<link>` tag. The `<link>` tag must be embedded in the `<head>` of your document and has the three main attributes:

- `rel`: Specifies the relationship between the linked document and the current one.
- `type`: Specifies the mime type of the linked document.
- `href`: Specifies the URL of the linked document.
- `media`: Specifies on what kind of device the linked document will be displayed.

Companion Site Reference

Example 3-1: Follow the link below to run this example on the companion site.

http://www.learnhtml5book.com/chapter3/basics1.php

An example of a linked CSS document for all media can be seen below:

```
<head>
<link rel="stylesheet" href="/css/basic.css" type="text/css" media="all">
</head>
```

As a side note, when documents are linked you can reduce the amount of data your browser will need to download via minification and gzip compression.

> ▓ **Note** Minification and compression allow you to shrink the content sent to the browser. So rather than sending a 100k CSS file to your browser the server sends a 3k css.gz (Gzip) file to your browser.

Mobile Safari supports compressed formats for both JavaScript and CSS files. You can search on "apache mod_deflate" as a means of automatically compressing CSS files.

@import

Another way to externalize your CSS files is to reference other CSS sheets from within a master stylesheet.

Companion Site Reference

Example 3-2: Follow the link below to run this example on the companion site.

```
http://www.learnhtml5book.com/chapter3/basics2.php
```

```
<style type="text/css">
  @import url("css/basic.css")  </style>
```

I would avoid using this if you can, mainly because of performance. It takes longer for the import method to render than the link tag.

Most of the CSS in the examples in this chapter can be found in the files sample.css and chapter3.css, except for Example 3-4, where I've put all the CSS in the main file so you can see it all side by side.

The Structure of CSS

CSS always has the following structure.

```
selector {property: value;}
```

- **Selectors** are alphanumeric and can be an element ID (#ID), an element className (.class), an element name (table), or a combination (h1.title).

- **Properties** identify what rule is being set. The list of properties is large, and includes things such as border, color, padding, margin, and the like.

- **Values** are assigned to each property. But only certain values are appropriate for certain elements and properties. So you would not be able to set the color to a value of 10 px (10 pixels).

CSS Browser Extensions

A lot of times in CSS you'll see strange prefixes in front of normal selectors; for example, instead of:

```
border-radius:10px;
```

you'll see:

```
-webkit-border-radius:10px;
```

These are called browser-specific extensions. The extensions for the browser rendering engines and their associated browsers are shown in Table 3-1.

Table 3-1. CSS Browser Extensions

Extension	Rendering Engine	Browsers
-ms-	Trident	Internet Explorer
-moz-	Mozilla	Firefox
-webkit-	Webkit	Safari, Mobile Safari, Chrome
-o-	Presto	Opera

■ **Special Extensions for Mobile Safari** There are almost a hundred –webkit extensions for iOS. One that you might want to use on your iOS device is –webkit-tap-highlight-color. This overrides the highlight color when a user taps a link or other clickable element.

You can get a complete list of –webkit extensions for iOS at a website called: CSS Infos. (http://css-infos.net /properties/webkit.php)

Media Queries and Media Selectors

If you can tell what device or media your site is being viewed on, you can use that information to assign a customized stylesheet. Back in HTML4 there were the following media types that could be listed as part of the <link> tag. So, for instance, you could assign different style rules for displaying your site on a TV screen versus a handheld device. These media types are still in use and they are:

- all
- aural
- braille
- handheld
- projection
- print
- screen
- tty
- tv

With HTML5, you can go a step further and specify rules within the media attribute to detect more specific information such as screen size and orientation. We access this information about the browser via a media query. The following tags are available.

- `width`
- `height`
- `device-width`
- `device-height`
- `orientation`
- `aspect-ratio`
- `device-aspect-ratio`
- `color`
- `color-index`
- `monochrome`
- `orientation`
- `resolution`
- `scan`
- `grid`
- `min-device-pixel-ratio`

The bold-face query properties in this list are the ones we use when determining whether we're on an iPhone, iPhone4 (Retina), or an iPad, so we use these later in the book.

orientation

This media query option allows you to link different CSS documents based on the orientation of your device. The two orientations available are portrait and landscape.

Companion Site Reference

Example 3-3: Follow the link below to run this example on the companion site.

`http://www.learnhtml5book.com/chapter3/orient.php`

For portrait you would use the following media query.

```
<link rel="stylesheet" media="all and (orientation:portrait)"  href="portrait.css">
```

Table 3-2. *Display sizes (portrait)*

Device	Device W × H	Working W × H
iPhone	320 × 480	320 × 356
iPhone4 (retina)	640 × 960	320 × 356*
iPad	768 × 1024	768 × 928

* See note on Retina Display

For landscape you would use the following media query.

```
<link rel="stylesheet" media="all and (orientation:landscape)" href="landscape.css">
```

Table 3-3. *Display sizes (landscape)*

Device	Device W × H	Working W × H
iPhone	480 × 320	480 × 208
iPhone4 (retina)	960 × 640	480 × 208*
iPad	1024 × 768	1024 × 672

* See note for Retina display.

So if you would like to change styles based on portrait or landscape, you would use an HTML header such as the following.

```
<head>
    <title>Some Title</title>
    <meta name="viewport" content="width=device-width" />
    <link rel="stylesheet" media="all and (orientation:portrait)"  href="portrait.css">
    <link rel="stylesheet" media="all and (orientation:landscape)" href="landscape.css">
</head>
```

Optionally you could create a single <link> to a CSS and then modify the CSS to contain the media query such as

```
header,nav,footer {border-radius:5px;border:1px solid #000;margin:5px;}
@media (orientation:portrait) {
    header {background-color:silver;color:black;}
}
@media (orientation:landscape) {
    header {background-color:black;color:silver;}
}
```

For my own app, the grandviewave mobile site, I've decided to use only portrait styles.

device-width

Although not mentioned above there are two additional subproperties of device-width. Those are: min-device-width, and max-device-width. The min-device-width for an iPhone is 320 px, because while in portrait orientation its width is 320 px and when in landscape it's 480 px.

You might think that an iPhone with Retina Display would show up differently, however, both the iPhone and iPhone4 give the same value from the media query.

```
@media screen and  (min-device-width: 320px) {…}
```

But because this query will also work for the iPhone4, you will need to use another media query to investigate the pixel ratio. This is a -webkit- specific property selector.

-webkit-min-device-pixel-ratio

So just as there are special extensions for webkit for CSS properties, there are also extensions for media queries. These will give you the ability to detect if you're on an iPhone or iPod Touch with a Retina Display.

```
<link rel="stylesheet" media="screen and (-webkit-min-device-pixel-ratio:2)"↩
 href="hires.css">
```

or

```
@media screen and (-webkit-min-device-pixel-ratio:2){
...
}
```

Now in order to tell if you are on each of the following it gets a little tricky because some of these will hold true for multiple media devices.

Media Selector Example

The first two media selectors highlight if the device is in portrait or landscape mode.
The third set of css properties sets the display of the <div> tags to none.
The remaining media queries select for the iPhone4, iPad, and iPhone, respectively.

Companion Site Reference

Example 3-4: Follow the link below to run this example on the companion site.

```
http://www.learnhtml5book.com/chapter3/iosselect.php
```

If you run this on the companion site, you'll see text highlighted that will tell you what device you're on and what orientation you're in.

```
<!doctype html>
<html>
<head>
<meta charset="utf-8">
<title>Some Title</title>
```

```
        <meta name="viewport" content="width=device-width" />
<style>

@media (orientation:portrait) {
        .portrait {display:block;}
        .landscape {display:none;}
}

@media (orientation:landscape) {
     .landscape {display:block;}
        .portrait {display:none;}
}
// default display none
.iphone4 {display:none;}
.iphone {display:none;}
.ipad {display:none;}
// iphone4
@media screen and (-webkit-min-device-pixel-ratio:2) {
     .iphone4 {display:block;}
}
// ipad
@media screen and (min-device-width: 768px){
     .ipad {display:block;color:green;}
}
// regular i
@media screen and (-webkit-max-device-pixel-ratio : 1.5) and (max-device-width: 480px){
     .iphone {display:block;}
}
</style>
</head>
<body>
<div class="landscape">Landscape</div>
<div class="portrait">Portrait</div>
<div class="ipad">iPad</div>
<div class="iphone">iPhone</div>
<div class="iphone4">iPhone4</div>
</body>
</html>
```

Normally you would put these in an external CSS, but I just put everything in one document so you can see it all together.

NOTE ON THE RETINA DISPLAY

The retina display is a little confusing. The iPhone media selectors still return a max-device-width of 480 px even though the device has a pixel count of 960 when in landscape mode.

With the Retina Display it's not the pixels on the screen that matter, it's the resolution or the DPI of those pixels. The DPI of the iPhone and iPod Touch is 163. The DPI of the Retina Display is 326. The DPI of the iPad is 132.

So how do you program this on your web app? Actually it's very easy. Let's say you want to display a 300 pixel image on the home page; rather than creating a 300 × 300 pixel image you just create a 600 × 600 pixel image then scale it down to 300 × 300 via the height and width properties of the image or a CSS rule for that element. Because of the pixel density, your 600 × 600 pixel image will be remarkably clear compared to the 300 pixel version.

You can view an example of this by going to the following page with your iPhone Retina Display or iPhone simulator (Retina). This is Example 3-5 on the companion site.

```
http://www.learnhtml5book.com/chapter3/retina.html
```

You can also find out more about the Retina Display on the Apple site.

Next we go over the important parts of CSS3 and iPhone-specific styling to make our app look and feel like a native app.

Saving to the Home Screen

In order to add your web app to the iOS home screen you will need four things.

- Home Screen Icon
- Start-Up/Splash Image
- Metatag for "Full Screen"
- Metatag for the style bar color

First we need to add some icons via specialized link and rel attributes.

```
<link rel="apple-touch-icon" href="/my-icon.png">
```

This icon will need to be 57 × 57 pixels for the iPhone, 114 × 114 for the iPhone (Retina), and 72 × 72 for the iPad.

This tells iOS to use my-icon.png as the icon for the home screen. Next we need to add a start-up image.

```
<link rel="apple-touch-startup-image" href="/startup-image.png">
```

This image will need to be 320 × 460 for the iPhone, 640 × 920 for the iPhone (Retina), and 768 × 1004 for the iPad Portrait, or 1024 × 748 for the iPad Landscape. This is the image that will be displayed on the start-up/splash screen when the web app loads.

Next we need to tell the web app to use the entire screen by removing the address bar and coloring the status bar. (We talked about these in Chapter 1.)

```
<meta name="apple-mobile-web-app-capable" content="yes" />
```

and

```
<meta name="apple-mobile-web-app-status-bar-style" content="black" />
```

There are three options for the content value (default, black, black-translucent).

Now in order to add your app to the home screen you just need to press the bookmark icon in the center of the Safari, or click the plus sign next to the address bar.

Figure 3-1. *Add to Home Screen*

A Short Overview of CSS3

Next I provide a short reference to CSS3. Mobile Safari supports most of these attributes natively so there's no need for the -webkit- prefix.

Animation

In CSS3 you can create animations without the need for Flash or JavaScript. To use animations you must use the CSS @keyframes rule, then specify the properties on the element that is doing the animation.

The example below sets the animation to run after two seconds and repeat forever. For example,

```
@-webkit-keyframes mytest {
  from {background: #ccc;} to {background: #000;}
 }
```

```
div {
  -webkit-animation-name: mytest;
  -webkit-animation-duration: 3s;
  -webkit-animation-timing-function: linear;
  -webkit-animation-delay: 2s;
  -webkit-animation-iteration-count: infinite;
  -webkit-animation-direction: alternate;
}
```

I can see animations being used when creating effects, and what's really nice is that it does not require JavaScript or a JavaScript framework like jQuery.

Backgrounds

There are a few changes as to how backgrounds are handled in CSS3 some of which will really help you when styling your iOS app.

Multiple Backgrounds

You can now specify multiple backgrounds for an element by adding comma-delimited background images.

```
background:url('img1.png'),url('img2.png');
```

You might typically use multiple backgrounds when you want a really nice effect or would like to combine a gradient with an image.

Clipping Backgrounds

This allows you to specify the painted area of the background of the element based on one of three settings:

- padding-box: Clipped to the padding
- border-box (the default): Clipped to the border
- content-box: Clipped to the content

```
background-clip:(content-box|border-box|content-box);
```

You would typically use the clipping property of a background when you need some customization on the placement of your background from within an element.

Background Origin

This specifies the positioning of the background image.

```
background-origin: padding-box|border-box|content-box;
```

As with clipping, you would typically use the origin property when you need to customize the placement of your background.

Background Size

This specifies the size of the background images.

```
background-size:width height;
```

In addition, it gives you the ability to resize a background just as you would do with an image.

Webkit Properties

There are also some webkit-based functions that allow you to create backgrounds dynamically, specifically, -webkit-gradient. For instance:

```
background: -webkit-linear-gradient(left, #ccc, #000);
```

This allows you to specify a linear gradient from top to bottom with the colors #ccc (gray) to #000 (black).

There are other webkit properties you can choose, each with a similar syntax.

Borders

With CSS3 you can add shadows to boxes, use an image as a border, or just round the edges.

Border Shadow

To create a shadow around an element use the following.

```
box-shadow: 5px 5px 5px #ccc;
```

The first two attributes are required. These are the horizontal and vertical positions of the shadow. Optionally you can select the blur distance, shadow size, shadow color, and if the shadow is outer or inner to the element.

Border Image

This allows you to use an image as a border.

```
border-image:url(border_img.png) 25 25 round;
```

Where the source is a url(), the image slice is the inward offset to the image, the width of the image border, or the outset of the border image beyond the border box, and repeat specifies whether it should be repeated, stretched, or rounded.

Rounded Borders

You can just simply round out the borders of your elements. You can also specify corners with border-top-left-radius, border-top-right-radius, border-bottom-left-radius, and border-bottom-right-radius.

```
border-radius:10px;
-webkit-border-radius-top-left:8px;
```

You would typically use this either by itself or with a custom selector to round part of an element (as within an iPhone-styled list shown later).

Fonts

Prior to CSS3 websites had to use the installed fonts on the user's computer. That's no longer the case; by creating the font-face rule you can specify the font to download. For example:

```
@font-face {
        font-family: testFont;
        src: url('myFont.ttf');
}

.class {
        font-family:testFont;
}
```

Additional font descriptors are:

- `font-stretch`: Normal (default), condensed, ultra-condensed, extra-condensed, semi-condensed, expanded, semi-expanded, extra-expanded, ultra-expanded

- `font-style`: Normal (default), italic, oblique

- `font-weight`: Normal (default), bold, 100–900

2D/3D Transforms

Now you can move, stretch, rotate, and scale elements via CSS. Some of the methods you can use on your elements are defined below.

Matrix

This combines all the transform methods into one by using six values that take the form of the top two rows, mathematically a 3 × 3 matrix.

A matrix of:

```
a b c
d e f
0 0 1
```

would take the form:

```
.class {
  transform: matrix (a,b,c,d,e,f);
  transform: matrix3d (a,b,c,d,e,f,g,h,i,j,k,l,m,n,o,p);
}
```

This gets rather complicated unless you're a math geek. Rather I move on to a few examples that are a little more intuitive. For 3D the matrix is 4 × 4 and has 16 values.

Rotate

This rotates an element.

```
.class {
  transform: rotate (45deg);
  transform: rotate3d (30,30,30,30deg);
}
```

Here you can rotate 2D by specifying the degrees of rotation, or for 3D you need to specify a unit vector of x, y, and z, followed by a degree of rotation.

Scale

This scales an element either larger or smaller and takes the form scale (1.5,2) which would increase the *x* component by 1.5 times and the *y* component by 2 times. You can also specify an individual axis with skewX, skewY, and skewZ. Or all three axes via scale3d(x,y,z).

Skew

Skew requires a little more imagination to comprehend. The following method skew(30deg,45deg) will rotate the element 30 degrees around the *x*-axis and 45 degrees around the *y*-axis.

Translate

This essentially moves your element by an *x*- and *y*-coordinate. You can either combine them or call them separately. An example takes the form:

```
.myClass {
  transform:translate(100px,100px); // 2d
  transform:translate3d(100px,100px,100px); // 3d
  transform:translateX(100px); // x coordinate
  transform:translateY(100px); // y coordinate
  transform:translate(100px); // z coordinate
}
```

Transitions

Transitions allow us to create an effect when transitioning from one style to the next. Let's say, for example, you're wanting to create a :hover effect on an element so that when the mouse is over an element you may change its color in some cases, or may even change its height or width.

The original element would be, let's say 50 pixels, but on :hover it might stretch to 100 pixels. Rather than having this element snap to 100 pixels we create a transition between element and element:hover.

You can either use the transition() property for everything, or you can use the properties individually.

- transition (property duration timing-function delay)

- transition-property: The name of the CSS property to which the transition is applied

- transition-duration: The duration of the transition

- transition-timing-function: The speed of the transition

- transition-delay: The delay before the transition starts

An example of use is:

```
.class {
  width:50px;
  transition: width 1s linear 2s;
}
.class:hover {
  width:100px;
}
```

Text Effects

There are many new text properties with CSS3; the ones we care most about when styling our iOS app are the text shadow and word wrap properties.

Text Shadow

The text shadow simply adds a shadow to the text with the following format,

```
text-shadow: horz-shadow vert-shadow blur color;
```

where the horz-shadow and vert-shadow represent the horizontal and vertical shadows, the blur represents the blur distance, and the color is the color of the shadow.

```
h1.title {text-shadow:2px 2px #ccc;}
```

Typically I would use a text shadow for text in a header or a button to give it a more native look and feel.

Word Wrap

This permits you to allow an element that might have unbreakable words broken so that content does not scroll unintentionally.

```
Article {word-wrap:break-word;}
```

There are other text properties defined in CSS3 including: hanging-punctuation, punctuation-trim, text-align-last, text-emphasis, text-justify, text-outline, text-overflow, text-wrap, and word-break.

This concludes a short reference of what's new in CSS3. Next we take what we've learned from CSS3 and apply it to making our ugly web app look like an iOS app.

Styling for iOS

Making our web app look like a native iPhone or iPad app is critical to its design. The main reason is that users are used to interacting with these devices in a certain way. Although you could make your application "work" without any iOS styling whatsoever, your adoption curve will take a serious hit.

What I do over the remainder of the chapter is show you how to perform some basic iOS styling techniques such as styling a list and button, or making use of the overflow and fixed positioning.

Styling a Header

All you need to do to create a header is add some CSS. I've added this to the file /chapter3/css/sample.css.

Companion Site Reference

Example 3-6: Follow the link below to run this example on the companion site.

```
http://www.learnhtml5book.com/chapter3/sample_header.php
```

```
header {
    text-align: center;
    height: 50px;
    background-image: -webkit-gradient(linear, left top, left bottom, from(#444), to(#000));
}

header h1 {
    color: #fff;
}
```

This will add a dark background with a gradient, and center an H1 with a white font.

Styling a List

Take a look at Figure 3-2. How do you make a list go from a plain list (on the left) to an iPhone-styled list (on the right)?

Figure 3-2. *Plain Navigation List (left) to iPhone-Styled List (right)*

Step 1: Create the HTML

First the HTML: I'm using the <nav>, <ul>, and <li> elements.

```
<nav>
<ul>
    <li class="arrow"><a href="">Businesses</a></li>
    <li class="arrow"><a href="">Near Me</a></li>
    <li class="arrow"><a href="">Sales &amp; Specials</a></li>
    <li class="arrow"><a href="">Parking</a></li>
    <li class="arrow"><a href="">Game</a></li>
    <li class="arrow"><a href="">Audio &amp; Video</a></li>
    <li class="arrow"><a href="">About</a></li>
    <li class="arrow"><a href="">Contact</a></li></ul>
</nav>
```

Step 2: Format the List

To format the <ul> and <li> elements I use the following CSS rules. I have added these to /chapter3/css/sample.css.

```
nav ul { // remove list style
    list-style:none;
    margin:10px;
    padding:0;
}
nav ul li a { // give some color and a border
    background-color:#fff;
    border: 1px solid #999;
    color:#222;
    display:block;
    font-weight:bold;
    margin-bottom:-1px;
    padding: 12px 10px;
    text-decoration:none;
}
nav ul.num2 li:first-child a { // create a rounded border on top
    border-top-left-radius:8px;
    border-top-right-radius:8px;
}
nav ul.num2 li:last-child a { // create a rounded border on the bottom
    border-bottom-left-radius:8px;
```

```
        border-bottom-right-radius:8px;
}
```

Step 3: Add the Chevron

Second we just need to add the chevron to the right of the image. For that I need to create a background image on the <a> tag because that's the element that was positioned. Then I just size the background and position it.

```
li.arrow a {
        background-image: url(chevron_36.png);
        background-size:22px;
        background-position: right center;
        background-position-x: 98%;
        background-position-y: 50%;
        background-repeat: no-repeat;
        background-repeat-x: no-repeat;
        background-repeat-y: no-repeat;
}
```

That's it. You can do more with the colors of the list and add transition effects, but we talk about that later on. Next we create a button.

Creating a Button

Now I show you how to convert a plain button (on the left of Figure 3-3) to an iPhone-styled button (on the right).

Companion Site Reference

Example 3-9: Follow the link below to run this example on the companion site.

http://www.learnhtml5book.com/chapter3/sample_buttons.php

Figure 3-3. Plain button and link (left) iPhone-styled button (right)

Step 1: Create the HTML

This is the basic HTML for Figure 3-3. You can see from the CSS below how you go from PLAIN to iOS.

```
<div style="padding:10px;">
<h2>Button</h2>
<button class="button">Checkout</button>
<h3>Links</h3>
<a href="sample_list2.php" class="back">Back</a><br>
</div>
```

Step 2: Size, Color, and Shadow the Buttons

This is the easy part; we just size and color the button and link, then apply a text-shadow to the text.

```
.button,.back {
    font-size:16px;
    line-height:18px;
    text-shadow: #333 1px 1px 2px;
    color:white;
    font-weight:bold;
    text-decoration:none;
    border-width:10px;
    padding:5px 10px;
}
```

Step 3: Add Border Images

Next I use the -webkit-border-image property to apply the round.png image to the border of the entire element. This means I can now stretch this image over the entire element. For the button, I just take a round image and stretch it until it fits the entire length of the text within the element. For the back button I need to do a little modification of the size so that it fits neatly inside the image.

```
.button {
    -webkit-border-image: url("round.png") 0 14 0 14 stretch;
}
.back {
    height:30px;
    line-height:14px;
    font-weight:normal;
    font-size:12px;
    padding:5px;
    color:#fff;
    -webkit-border-image: url("back.png") 0 14 0 14 stretch;
}
```

Overflow (iOS5)

In versions previous to iOS5 you had to perform a three-finger swipe to activate an area with overflow. This made it very difficult or impossible to get fixed positioning of elements from within the window of Mobile Safari but, more important, it was not intuitive.

iPhone Fixed Footer Example

All you need to do now is measure your working area and add the overflow properties to your element.

```
nav {
    height: 250px;
    overflow-y: auto;
    -webkit-overflow-scrolling:touch;
}

footer {
    position: absolute;
    top: 300;
    border: 1px solid red;
```

```
    width: 300px;
    margin: 10px;
    height: 40px;
}
```

The example above creates an overflow for the navigation and a fixed footer.

iPad Split View Example

Here's an example on the iPad of how to create a split-view page. This allows you to take the navigation and put it on the left 30% of the page and then take the main content and display it on the right 70%. You can even add the overflow and `webkit-content-scrolling` properties to the `<nav>` element to give it a more native look and feel.

In Figure 3-4 I've added a border and a few more contact links to show you how it is scrolling on an iPad. When you touch this part of the screen it actually shows you a scrollbar as you're moving your finger.

Companion Site Reference

Example 3-10: Follow the link below to run this example on the companion site.

```
http://www.learnhtml5book.com/chapter3/ipad.php
```

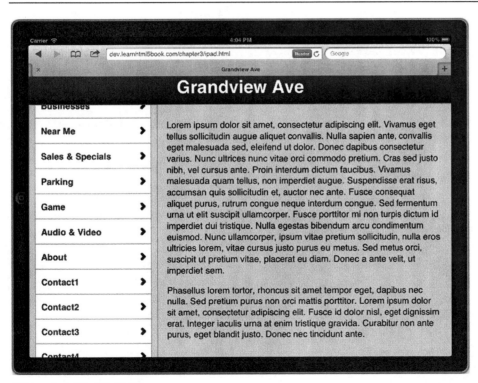

Figure 3-4. *iPad Split View*

Putting It All Together

We left off with the Grandview Web App in a rather ugly state. It was nothing more than some HTML5 mark-up and a few ideas about how we wanted the navigation to work. But now thanks to CSS3 we can start to make it look like a native iPhone or iPad app.

There are two main things we want to take from this section and apply to your app: device and orientation selection and how to make our web app act like an app and add it to our home screen.

Device and Orientations

You can have up to six different combinations of devices and orientations for your mobile web app. For Grandview Ave I just pick two: iPhone Portrait and iPad Landscape. I also add a special selector for Retina Display devices so that the images and icons that I use can have twice the resolution.

I chose these two after reviewing the log statistics from my site and finding that those two profiles were responsible for over 90% of my mobile views. Because of this I won't need to create a separate stylesheet and I also don't want to incur the additional network call. I just put everything in a single stylesheet called grandviewave.css like this:

```
<link rel="stylesheet" href="/css/grandviewave.css" type="text/css" media="all">
```

This means that I need to create the following media selectors.

```
/** iphone **/
@media screen and (-webkit-max-device-pixel-ratio : 1.5) and (max-device-width: 480px){
}
/** iphone 4 **/
@media screen and (-webkit-min-device-pixel-ratio:2) {
}
/** ipad **/
@media screen and (min-device-width: 768px){
}
```

With these media selectors I can have a common area of CSS at the top and the device-specific selectors down below within the media query sections defined above.

Full Screen Web App

Next because I want to add my app as a full-screen web app I need to add the metatags and images to my site. I use the <meta> tags to say this is web app capable and then use the <link> tags in combination with the media selectors to pick the right images.

```
<link rel="apple-touch-startup-image"
media="(max-device-width: 480px) and not (-webkit-min-device-pixel-ratio: 2)"
href="iphone.png" />

<link rel="apple-touch-startup-image"
media="(max-device-width: 480px) and (-webkit-min-device-pixel-ratio: 2)"
href="iphone4.png" />

<link rel="apple-touch-startup-image"
media="(max-device-width: 1024px) and (orientation: portrait)"
href="ipad-portrait.png" />
```

```
<link rel="apple-touch-startup-image"
media="(max-device-width: 1024px) and (orientation: landscape)"
href="ipad-landscape.png" />
```

The remaining item I need to finish (in addition to the content and data) is the navigation. I put the finishing touches on that in Chapter 6.

Chapter Summary

In this chapter I gave you an overview of CSS3 and iPhone-/iPad-specific media-kit-based rendering tricks to make your web app look like a native iPhone or iPad app.

This list is not comprehensive. In fact for Grandview Ave I actually use a Mobile Framework discussed in Chapter 5, but what you've learned in this chapter will allow you to roll your own mobile framework or modify an existing one.

Before moving on to the next chapter you should know how to do the following.

- Externalize your CSS.

- Use Media Queries to better customize your CSS for properties such as orientation or device-width.

- Save your iPhone or iPad web app to the home screen.

- Use some of the basics of the new features in CSS3.

- Style a native-looking list and buttons.

- Take advantage of overflow for iOS 5.

Now that we know how to make your web app look good, it's time to talk about how to make it functional and get data from our web site. That will involve JavaScript and that's what I talk about next.

C H A P T E R 4

JavaScript and APIs

There's a lot to know about JavaScript and the APIs of HTML5. So much so it's not really possible to go over everything. However, there's a lot we can cover that's important to mobile development. Many of the things I talk about can be achieved by using a JavaScript framework such as jQuery, which is introduced at the end of the chapter, but first you need to know the basics of what's under the hood so you can deviate from a framework or fix problems when they come up.

The first thing to look at is the basics of JavaScript: things such as how to include and reference external JavaScript files as well as some basics for creating JavaScript objects and methods. Next I go into some of the JavaScript events you'll use over and over.

Finally I talk about how to roll your own AJAX objects and a little about JSON (JavaScript Object Notation) for retrieving remote data. We use PHP to handle the remote data in Grandview Ave, but you could use HTML, Ruby, JSON, Python, .NET, anything really. The important thing is that we're getting remote data and bringing them in via AJAX.

Before getting into the APIs and items above, I will stray a little bit into the history of JavaScript because the structure of the language is vital to everything we want to do and it's especially important when comparing JavaScript to a server-side language.

About JavaScript

JavaScript is a unique language. I will give you a little bit of an overview of JavaScript because I think it goes a long way in understanding the way frameworks and things work in JavaScript as compared to Objective-C, C, C++, Java, Ruby, PHP, or .C# languages. When frameworks break or a problem comes up, many web developers get stuck because they ignore much of this information.

JavaScript was originally developed by Brendan Eich of Netscape in 1995, and is an implementation of the ECMAScript language standard. Other dialects of ECMAScript include Jscript and ActionScript. The current edition of ECMAScript is 5 and the current JavaScript version is 1.8.5.

JavaScript is a *scripting language*. Scripting languages control one or more applications. There are many types of scripting languages. Some are for shells such as bash or batch files. Other languages including Perl started out as scripting languages but became more powerful. But because scripting languages by definition control one or more applications, JavaScript controls the web browser application.

JavaScript is dynamic as opposed to static. Dynamic languages are a class of programming languages that execute at runtime and can change their composition while running. This is more than just modifying the state of certain variables: dynamic languages can add code and extend objects, all during the course of program execution making the distinction between code and data difficult.

JavaScript is weakly typed as opposed to strongly typed. Weakly typed languages essentially just allow you to not specify the type for a variable. So the variable foo can be set to an integer, a string, a double, or an array and can change during the course of program execution.

JavaScript is object-oriented. This is a style of programming performed with objects or complex data structures that are composed of variables and methods. Those variables and methods provide an object with certain behavior.

JavaScript is prototype-based. Prototype-based means that you create objects by cloning other objects rather than instantiating objects from a class (template).

JavaScript is a functional language. A functional language is one that treats computer programs similar to mathematical functions. This is a 10-dollar word for a 10-cent concept. Basically it just means that if you pass a variable to a function, it returns another variable. All states are contained within the function's input variables.

JavaScript has first-class functions. A first-class function basically means you can pass in a function to another function. This can best be seen in the example below.

Companion Site Reference

Example 4-1: Follow the link below to run this example on the companion site.

```
http://www.learnhtml5book.com/chapter4/jsfunction.php
```

```
// normal function
function foo(a, b) { return a + b; }
// normal function as variable
var foo2 = function(a,b) { return a+b; }
// function as parameter to another function
function foo3(foo2,a,b) {
    return foo2(a,b);
}
// outputs 3,3,3
alert(foo(1,2)+","+foo2(1,2)+","+foo3(foo2,1,2));
```

Based on your style of programming and background you may prefer to use an object-oriented approach or a functional approach. This is known as *multiparadigm*. Some JavaScript libraries might be entirely function-based, whereas others will be more object-oriented. Either way there's a lot to learn about the language; next I talk about a few useful parts.

Using JavaScript

There's a lot to talk about in JavaScript. I recommend getting one of the fine Apress books on just JavaScript by itself to learn all the ins and outs of the language. But in lieu of that I touch on some of the most useful parts of the language, specifically the parts we need for creating our mobile web app.

Externalizing JavaScript

Just as in Chapter 3 when we externalized, minified, and gzipped CSS, we can do the same with JavaScript.
Inline JavaScript would look like this:

```
<script type="text/javascript">
function foo() {...}
</script>
```

Externalized JavaScript would look like this:

```
<script type="text/javascript" src="external.js"></script>
```

It's important to note that JavaScript executes as soon as it's loaded, so the order of loading is important. If you have two JavaScript files and one is dependent on the other, say you have function foo() in external.js, you can't call foo before it's loaded; you'll get an object not found error.

Creating Objects and Using Namespaces

There are a few ways to design a JavaScript library: one is to create a bunch of global functions, and another is to create JavaScript objects or namespaces for your custom functions. Take a look at the following example.

Companion Site Reference

Example 4-2: Follow the link below to run this example on the companion site.

```
http://www.learnhtml5book.com/chapter4/objects.php
```

```
var a = 0;
function add_a() {
        a=a+1;
}
add_a();
add_a();
alert("a = " + a);

function something() {
        a = "a string";
}
something();
alert("a = " + a);
```

In the example above, the global variable a starts off as an integer, and ends up as a string. Now imagine if this function or global variable were used inside an external library or rather what if you had name collisions from two different external libraries? This would get quite difficult to debug. To avoid this we create objects or use namespaces.

■ **Note** The variable $ is used by many JavaScript frameworks including jQuery. Make sure you don't use this variable if you're using a JavaScript framework.

```
var b = new Object();
b.count = 0;
b.add = function() {
```

```
        this.count = this.count+1;
}
b.add();
b.add();
alert("b = "+b.count);
```

In the above example, we just create an object and set a property of count on that object and increment it by the method add.

Now we can do whatever we want to b and it will just be for b and we don't need to worry about this unless b is a global variable used in an external library that we've imported. As you can see the method of creating objects is rather easy; you just need to declare a variable as an object and then add properties to it, followed by methods (functions).

Events

Events are actions that can be detected such as scrolling your window, clicking a button, or focusing on an element. I talk about a few below that you'll want to make use of when building your mobile web app.

The first events I talk about are how to recognize when your page is done being loaded, because most of the time this is when you'll want to start doing things.

window.onload and DOMContentLoaded

I have not been able to tell the difference in timing between the two, but don't use window.onload, even if you're just using mobile safari. The reason is that some browsers fire the window.onload event when everything is loaded just like document.body.onload, but mobile safari seems to fire this event when the DOM is ready.

The preferred method of checking to see whether the DOM is ready for manipulation is to check to see if it's loaded. You can do that via the following event handler function.

```
document.addEventListener('DOMContentLoaded', domready());
```

If you are using external JavaScript or waiting for images to load so you can manipulate them, this event will fire too early. In these cases, you'll want to use the onload attribute in the <body> tag instead.

body.onload

The body.onload event fires when all of the items on a page are finished loading. This means all external files including CSS, JavaScript, and Images.

■ **Note** Be careful when calling third-party APIs. The onload event will not fire until these are done loading, which could take some time.

The following example demonstrates the difference in timing between body onload and DOMContentLoaded by printing an alert when each event occurs. Because of the speed of today's browsers I've used a 10-megabyte image file to slow things down.

Companion Site Reference

Example 4-3: Follow the link below to run this example on the companion site.

http://www.learnhtml5book.com/chapter4/load.php

```
<body onload="bodyload()">
<img src="10megfile.jpg">
</body>
<script type="text/javascript">
document.addEventListener('DOMContentLoaded', domready());
function bodyload() {
    alert('body load');
}
function domready() {
    alert('dom ready');
}
</script>
</body>
```

▓ **Note** The iOS is limited to 10-megabyte files for images, CSS, or other resources. Make sure you limit your files to this size otherwise they will not be downloaded.

window.onhashchange

What's the hash? Well the hash is the part of your URL after the # sign. So if your URL is http://domain.com/resource.php#123, the location.hash would be 123. This is a useful feature when you are using the location.hash as a means of maintaining state on your web page and you're dynamically loading parts of the page via AJAX.

In the URL Example http://domain.com/business.php#123, the 123 could be the primary key in the database row of businesses. If your user clicked the back button and it was 122, you might want to load the content again for business 122.

Before JavaScript included this event we had to create a timer that would look for changes in the location.hash value every few hundred milliseconds.

window.onorientationchange

In Chapter 3 we showed you how to detect your browser's orientation via a media query in the <link> tag. But what if you want to do more with your app besides change the style of the web page? Well, you use this event window.onorientationchange.

```
window.onorientationchange = function() {
    alert("orientation = " + window.orientation);
}
```

The following are the orientation values and position of the iOS device.

- 0 – Portrait mode
- 90 – Landscape mode (button on the right)
- –90 – Landscape mode (button on the left)

The orientation does not read upside-down orientations (button on the top).

Dialogs

The following three dialog types work in iOS (see Figure 4.1).

- alert(string) – This returns a void and allows the user to press OK to acknowledge the alert. You might use this to display simple confirmation messages or feedback to your user.
- confirm(string) – This also displays a message but returns a true if OK is clicked and a false if Cancel is clicked. You might use this to ask for Boolean feedback, without the fanciness of an HTML dialog.
- prompt(string) – This also displays a message but returns a string depending on what the user has entered. You might use this in place of an HTML form for simple input.

Figure 4-1. Different dialogs as displayed on the iPhone

I often use the alert box to show some debugging information, but there's another way to get even more detailed information and that's by using the JavaScript console.

Safari JavaScript Console

First and foremost make sure your debugging console is turned on (see Chapter 1, Figure 1-2).
Next there are four kinds of messages that will appear on your debugging console:

- *log* – General log messages
- *info* – Informational messages
- *warning* – Warnings that do not cause breakage
- *error* – Errors that could cause the page to break and stop working.

Companion Site Reference

Example 4-6: Follow the link below to run this example on the companion site.

`http://www.learnhtml5book.com/chapter4/console.php`

You can see how those messages look in the code below and in Figure 4-2.

```
console.log("this is a log message");
console.info("this is an info message");
console.warn("this is a warning message");
console.error("this is an error message");
```

Figure 4-2. Console messages

Creating an API

When creating an API it's important to think how you're going to use it. For our app, Grandview Ave, I use it for two things, simplifying application design for multiple devices and to publish data to multiple web sites and apps. Let's list these below.

Device-Centric Usage

- Mobile iPad site
- Mobile iPhone site
- Other mobile site (Android and Blackberry)
- Native iPhone app
- Native iPad app
- Native Android app

Data-Centric Usage

- Publish HTML content to mobile site
- Publish business category data
- Publish business detail data
- Sales and specials
- Near Me functionality
- Parking data

The back-end for your API can be anything you want; for my examples I use PHP to create a RESTful web service or API.

■ **REST (Representation State Transfer)** REST basically means that you have a URL where you can GET, PUT, POST, and DELETE data. The URL defines the data, and the methods define what you want to do with them.

An example could be: `http://domain.com/resource.html` or

`http://domain.com/resource/business.php?id=1`.

Once you lay out the URLs and files you're going to use to provide these data to your mobile site or app, you'll need a way to get the data, and we do that with AJAX.

Getting Remote Data with AJAX

AJAX stands for Asynchronous JavaScript and XML and it was first implemented by Microsoft in Internet Explorer 5 as an ActiveX object named XMLHttpRequest. The idea behind this was simple: provide rich functionality to a browser by requesting XML from a URL and then parsing this XML on the browser with VBScript or JavaScript to spice up the interface so developers would not need to run ActiveX or Java in their browsers.

This object was later added to Safari and has the syntax:

```
var httpReq = new XMLHttpRequest();
```

The XMLHttpRequest object has the following methods.

- `open(method(GET | POST), url, true(asynchronous) | false (synchronous), username, password)` – Opens the request and makes the request if a GET
- `send()` – Sends the request
- `abort()` – Cancels the current request
- `getAllResponseHeaders()` – Returns all HTTP headers as a string
- `setRequestHeaders(label,value)` – Sets the request headers to be sent in the request

This object also has an event listener called onreadystatechange; this event fires for each of the ready states below:

- 0 – Uninitialized.
- 1 – Opened, but send not called.
- 2 – Opened, send has been called.
- 3 – Receiving; this is when response is being downloaded.
- 4 – Loaded, or finished receiving response.

The object also has the following properties containing the downloaded response.

- `responseText` – Just a string of the response.
- `responseXML` – The response as XML.
- `responseBody` – The response as a binary encoded string.
- `status` – The status code of the response: 200 indicates OK; 404 would be "file not found".
- `statusText` – The status text such as "not found" or "ok".

Here's a simple AJAX example that makes a call to a local file called simple.txt, and it will alert the contents of this file to the screen.

Companion Site Reference

Example 4-7: Follow the link below to run this example on the companion site.

`http://www.learnhtml5book.com/chapter4/ajax.php`

```
var req = new XMLHttpRequest();
var url = "sample.txt";
req.open("GET", url);
req.onreadystatechange =  function() {
    if (req.readyState == 4) {
        var txt = req.responseText;
        alert(txt);
    }
};
req.send();
```

Since AJAX was invented there have been other kinds of data in addition to XML that have been sent back via `XMLHttpRequest`: Plain Text, HTML, CSV (Comma Separated Values), and JSON (JavaScript Object Notation).

It's also important to note that all the major JavaScript frameworks use this object for their AJAX functions.

Response Data Matrix

Table 4-1 shows a few sample data types with pros and cons of each.

Table 4-1. Pros and Cons of Different Response Data

Data Type	Mime Type	Pro	Con
Plain Text	text/Plain	Simple, good for simple messages.	Not readily parsed for complicated data types.
HTML	text/HTML	Good for injecting as dynamic content.	Not good for data as its markup is not descriptive.
CSV	text/CSV	Good for tables or large lists.	Not well suited for hierarchical data.
XML	text/XML	Can suit flat or hierarchical data, easily parsed.	Quite verbose and deeply nested data structures require lots of syntax to get a single item.
JSON	application/JSON	It's JavaScript, not as verbose as XML, and can easily map to existing objects or flat data structures.	Requires separate decorating markup, as this is just data and structure.

I think that each of these return types has its place in a RESTful API, but next we need to understand a little bit more about JSON.

JSON (JavaScript Object Notation)

JSON is basically structured text that transmits data in a form easily digestible and evaluated by JavaScript using `eval()` or `JSON.parse()`. Although most of the time you end up using JSON with JavaScript, it's actually a language-independent data format like XML or YML. For a detailed overview of JSON, Wikipedia has a nice example comparing it to XML: http://en.wikipedia.org/wiki/JSON

■ **Note** Although you could use the `eval()` method for evaluating JSON text, this makes your application vulnerable to injection or kinds of attacks. `JSON.parse()` is the new JSON object available as a safer alternative to `eval`.

When thinking about JSON just think of it as a class or an object but without a name. So rather than creating a class named Person, with properties of id and name, just create the object with those properties; it can be named whatever you want it to be.

Companion Site Reference

Example 4-8: Follow the link below to run this example on the companion site.

```
http://www.learnhtml5book.com/chapter4/json.php
```

```
{
    "id" : 1,
    "name": "Scott"
}
```

Then to evaluate or parse this object (named JSON) just follow the steps below.

```
var json = '{"id":1,"name":"Scott"}';
var obj1 = eval("("+json+")");
var obj2 = JSON.parse(json);
alert(obj1.name + ", id= " + obj2.id);
```

JSON has the following basic types.

- String
- Number
- Boolean
- Array
- Object
- Null or Empty

JSON does not support the following native types.

- Date
- Error
- Math
- Regular expressions
- Function

So although it's JavaScript, it's best for representing JavaScript data, and that means you will not need to parse XML. Now that we can get JSON or HTML data from our API how do we get it on the page? That's where DOM manipulation comes into play.

DOM Manipulation

Before HTML5 if you wanted to work with an element you would need to use the trusty `getElementById` method.

```
<div id="foo"></div>
<script>
var elt = document.getElementById("foo");
elt.innerHTML = "this is cool";
</script>
```

If you recall in Chapter 2 I talked about some new selectors made possible by HTML5; you could select this same element or you could select by either a class name or an id, or something else.

```
<div id="foo"></div>
<div class="someclass"></div>
<script>
var elt1 = document.getElementsByClassName("someclass");
var elt2 = document.querySelector("#foo");
</script>
```

Now once you have an element you can manipulate it in many ways; usually you'll change its style or modify its contents.

```
<script>
var elt = document.getElementById("foo");
elt.innerHTML = "this is cool";
elt.style.color = "red";
elt.className = "newClass";
</script>
```

When you combine AJAX, JSON, and DOM manipulation you get an externalized data file in the form of JSON, retrieved through AJAX (`XMLHttpRequest`) and populated on the page via DOM manipulation.

In the example below I have to use placeholder `<span>` tags populated from a JSON file requested through AJAX.

Companion Site Reference

Example 4-9: Follow the link below to run this example on the companion site.

```
http://www.learnhtml5book.com/chapter4/combo.php
```

```
ID: <span id="id"></span><br>
Name: <span id="name"></span>

<script>
    var req = new XMLHttpRequest();
    var url = "sample.json";
    var nameElt = document.getElementById("name");
    var idElt = document.getElementById("id");
    var obj;
```

```
        req.open("GET", url);
        req.onreadystatechange =  function() {
                if (req.readyState == 4) {
                        var json = req.responseText;
                        obj = JSON.parse(json);
                        idElt.innerHTML = obj.id;
                        nameElt.innerHTML = obj.name;
                }
        };
        req.send();
</script>
```

■ **Note** Keep in mind that safari follows HTTP/1.1 and allows only four concurrent requests at a time, meaning that if you have five objects on a page, the fifth object will be loaded once the first one is finished from the first four.

Creating Elements and Adding Events

Another way to inject HTML into a document is just to create it with JavaScript. This has some benefit if you don't want to create the HTML from a JSON returned from an AJAX request.

This is an example of creating a red `<div>` with an `onclick` event handler that creates an alert box.

Companion Site Reference

Example 4-10: Follow the link below to run this example on the companion site.

http://www.learnhtml5book.com/chapter4/creating.php

```
<body></body>
<script>
    var elt = document.createElement("div");
    elt.onclick = function () {alert("new element")};
    elt.style.border = "1px solid red";
    elt.style.width = "200px";
    elt.style.height = "200px";
    elt.innerHTML = "click me";
    document.body.appendChild(elt);
</script>
```

All of this is done with JavaScript and this kind of functionality will come in very handy later on.

JavaScript Frameworks

Up until now we've been doing everything manually: selecting the elements from the DOM we want to work with, adding our event handlers, creating XMLHttpRequest objects, and looking for their ready state to fire off events. But there's another way to do this, which I mentioned back at the start of this chapter.

There are a bunch of great developers doing all this work so you don't need to! I'm talking about JavaScript Frameworks.

What's a JavaScript Framework?

A JavaScript framework is more than just a library that allows you to do Ajax or has UI widgets; it has a full stack of functionality, for example:

- Cross browser support
- Ajax support
- DOM manipulation and traversal
- Event handling
- JSON
- Selectors
- Animation and effects

So you won't need to code any of this yourself. And in addition, you will find that more developers know how to create a jQuery Ajax request than know how to create an XMLHttpRequest object and wait for the result to pass to a function.

▓ **Note** The Magic Dollar Sign $: All of the frameworks use a special character or words to denote usage of this object/function. For jQuery, Prototype, and MooTools it's a dollar sign $, Yahoo! UI uses YAHOO and ExtJS uses Ext.

Some of the most popular JavaScript Frameworks include:

- **jQuery** – The most popular JavaScript framework and talked about more in subsequent pages.
- **Prototype** – A very popular framework created by Sam Stephenson in February of 2005.
- **MooTools** – Originally an extension of the Prototype framework created by Valerio Proietti in September of 2006.
- **YUI** – The Yahoo! user interface library created in 2005 for use in creating user interface components.
- **ExtJS** – Originally created as an extension to YUI, it also includes interoperability with jQuery and Prototype.

jQuery

jQuery was first released in January 2006 by John Resig and is the most popular JavaScript framework in use today. We use this framework throughout the book. jQuery is free and open sourced, and dual licensed under MIT License and GPL v2.

The current version of jQuery is 1.6.2 and it has a zipped size of 31Kb, and a minified size of 84K. The web site for learning more about jQuery is http://jquery.com.

To get jQuery to work all you need to do is download it from the web site and place it on your page like in the example below.

Companion Site Reference

Example 4-11: Follow the link below to run this example on the companion site.

http://www.learnhtml5book.com/chapter4/jquery.php

```
<script type="text/javascript" src="jquery-1.6.2.min.js"></script>
<script type="text/javascript">
$().ready(function(){
    alert("jquery ready");
 });

</script>
```

jQuery uses the syntax $(). This is the selector function to the jQuery library. Inside the () you put a "selector" where a selector can be a CSS-style selector such as "#id" or ".class", or even an entire element type "a". An empty selector defaults to document so $() is the same as $(document).

After the selector you have methods that range from ready() for determining if the document is ready, to effects such as hide or show.

Putting It All Together

Previously we figured out how to take a normal HTML page and frame it, style it, and use some HTML5 tags to organize it, but it's still just a shell. The steps we need to take from this chapter are:

- Creating a data API to access server data

- Using Ajax to retrieve and populate the pages of our mobile app

- Using the jQuery JavaScript framework for all the heavy work

Let's look again at the data that we want to get from our API. Table 4-2 outlines our API components along with their data types and URLs. I've used PHP to retrieve server-side data for Grandview Ave, but you can use anything you want in your own apps, even HTML.

Table 4-2. API Overview of GrandviewAve

API Component	Data Type	Resource
Business Categories	List/JSON or HTML	/api/categories.php
Business List	List/JSON or HTML	/api/list.php?catid
Business Details	JSON or HTML	/api/detail.php?busid

API Component	Data Type	Resource
Business Near Me	List/JSON or HTML	/api/nearme.php?latlong
Sales and Specials	List/JSON or HTML	/api/sales.php
Parking	List/JSON or HTML	/api/parking.php
The Avenue Hunt	TBD	—
Audio and Video	TBD	—
About	HTML	/api/about.php
Contact	Text	/api/contact.php

So far my directory structure looks like that shown in Figure 4-3.

Figure 4-3. Current GrandviewAve directory structure

I've got HTML files and I've put the associated PHP files that will handle the data in the /api directory. You could put everything in the same location and just have .php files for everything, but I'm organizing it like this because I will need the data-only parts in Chapter 15 when we convert Grandview

Ave to a native app. Now to bring in the data for an example page, say about.html, I need to add some code like this.

```
<!doctype html>
<html>
<meta charset="utf-8">
<head>
<title>About Grandview Ave</title>
<meta name="viewport" content="width=device-width" />
<script type="text/javascript" src="/js/jquery-1.6.2.min.js"></script>
<script type="text/javascript">

$().ready(function(){
        $("#about").load('/api/about.php').delay(500).fadeIn('slow');
});

</script>
</head>
<body>
<div id="about" style="display:none;"></div>
</body>
</html>
```

When you run this page in the 'Putting It All Together' section on the companion site, you'll see I've added a 500-millisecond delay and decided to fade-in the content slowly.

Now if this is not HTML and I want to bring in JSON for the list of categories, I might do something such as this, with a JSON formatted PHP page returning dynamic data called categories.php. This is the next example on the companion site.

```
<!doctype html>
<html>
<meta charset="utf-8">
<head>
<title>Categories</title>
<meta name="viewport" content="width=device-width" />
<script type="text/javascript" src="/js/jquery-1.6.2.min.js"></script>
<script type="text/javascript">

    $().ready(function(){
       $.getJSON('/api/categories.php', function(data) {
        var items = [];
          $.each(data, function(key, val) {
            items.push('<li id="' + key + '">' + val + '</li>');
        });
      $('<ul/>', {
        'class': 'my-new-list',
        html: items.join(")
        }).appendTo('#cats');
        });
    });

</script>
</head>
<body>
<div id="cats"></div>
```

```
</body>
</html>
```

Now iterating through the JSON is a little more complicated than just returning the HTML. You might find that creating the HTML in JavaScript is a little awkward. If that's the case then just create HTML from your API and return it.

Now because I don't want to have all of my JavaScript on each page I need to externalize it and create some functions and device detection variables.

```
<script type="text/javascript" src="/js/grandviewave.js"></script>
```

Note that I put the grandviewave.js file after jQuery. This is very important because there are dependencies on jQuery and your page could show errors if reversed. So far my external JavaScript looks like this.

/js/grandviewave.js as of Chapter 4

```
var isiPhone = navigator.userAgent.match(/iPhone/i);
var isiPod = navigator.userAgent.match(/iPod/i);
var isiPad = navigator.userAgent.match(/iPad/i);

window.onhashchange = function() {}
window.onorientationchange = function() {}
function load_content() {
    var url = document.location.toString();
    if (url.match(/about/i)) {
        $("#content").load('/api/about.php');
    }
    if (url.match(/index/i)) {
        $("#content").load('/api/categories.php');
    }
    // .. do for remainder of pages
}

// will use this for all load events
$().ready(function(){
    load_content();
});
```

So far we have placeholders for onHashChange and onOrientationChange as well as some preliminary loading content steps based on the URL. We can load the contents of each .html page with the associated API data page (about.php). The page /api/about.php will just provide plain HTML derived from the site's Content Management System.

Chapter Summary

In this chapter we talked about how to create an API and some basics of JavaScript such as Ajax and DOM manipulation. Some of the items (including the XMLHttpRequest object or document.querySelector) you might never use because you'll be using a JavaScript framework such as jQuery.

Nevertheless, if you find yourself debugging a framework, or wanting to just experiment, I thought it would be nice to show you what's underneath the covers of a powerful framework such as jQuery because nothing is worse than being dependent on something about which you know little.

Before moving on to the next chapter you should know how to:

- Create and structure your data API.

- Have an idea for what kind of data your API will use: HTML, XML, Plain Text, JSON, or a combination.

- Know how to retrieve these data via AJAX using either `XMLHttpRequest` or jQuery.

- Know how to display these data on your page via DOM manipulation either manually or via jQuery.

- Know where to find some useful information on events, debugging, and dialogs.

But still we don't have styling or any cool effects and it might take a long time to code them, so although jQuery is great and saves us a lot of time there's still a piece missing. This is why we need to talk about mobile frameworks next.

CHAPTER 5

Mobile Frameworks

Mobile frameworks put together three things.

- Common JavaScript APIs and libraries
- CSS and themes (natively styled)
- Effects

So although we did all this work by ourselves in the previous chapters, now we have a mobile framework that will do most of the work for us. In this chapter I talk about jQuery Mobile. There are other Mobile Web Frameworks out there such as iUI, Sencha Touch, jQTouch, and iWebKit to name a few. They all do basically the same thing: give you a CSS and JS framework for making your mobile web apps look and feel like a native app. Or in some cases provide you the ability to convert your web app to a native app via a framework such as Phonegap (which I talk about in Chapter 15).

Although we're focused on iPhone and iPad apps it's worth noting that jQuery Mobile supports Blackberry, Android, Palm, and Windows phones. So should you want to expand your mobile footprint you won't need to do much and if you already know jQuery the learning curve is rather small. By the end of the chapter we'll be ready to code the home page of our sample web app, Grandview Avenue.

Companion Site Reference

Example 5-1: Follow this link to see an alternative mobile framework in action (iUI).

```
http://www.learnhtml5book.com/chapter5/iui/index.html
```

Overview of jQuery Mobile

To get a basic jQuery mobile page you will need three things:

- Latest copy of jQuery – (http://jquery.com)
- Latest copy of jQuery Mobile CSS
- Latest copy of jQuery Mobile JS

> ■ **Note** At the time of writing this book the current version of jQuery Mobile is 1.0 beta3.

To use jQuery Mobile on your page, the <head> of your document should look like the code below.

Companion Site Reference

Example 5-2: Follow the link below to run this example on the companion site.

http://www.learnhtml5book.com/chapter5/jquerymobile/index.html

```
<head>
 <title>JQuery Mobile</title>
 <meta name="viewport" content="width=device-width" />
 <link rel="stylesheet" href="jquery.mobile-1.0b3.min.css" />
 <script src="jquery-1.6.4.min.js"></script>
 <script src="jquery.mobile-1.0b3.min.js"></script>
</head>
```

> ■ **Note** You will need to add location prefixes to the href and src attributes, depending on your directory structure. The example assumes that everything is in the same directory.

In the next sections I talk about the details of jQuery mobile. You can find out more from http://jquerymobile.com.

Working with Pages

The first thing to discuss is some of the conventions associated with the page structure. These are the rules that allow the framework to do things as intended. These rules consist of CSS class names, element IDs, and structural conventions. So although you might think you can just name some stuff according to the class names or ID names, if you're missing the structure, things won't work.

This is because this mobile framework (actually all mobile frameworks) in order to be efficient uses nested CSS selectors for layout and CSS element selectors in the JS logic to do certain things. If you don't follow a convention rule the framework might not work and therefore your page won't work.

> ■ **Note** *Convention over Configuration* is a design paradigm that allows programmers to stick to a set of rules rather than making decisions about how their code needs to be configured. jQuery Mobile, like many of today's frameworks, uses this design approach.

I suggest that if you want to modify the convention, that's fine; just use the convention first, then tweak and test as you go rather than creating something you want and trying to do it the other way around.

Page Data-Role

The first meta-element attribute you'll use is `data-role`. This tells the framework that the contents of the element should be a page.

What's a Page?

The term page can be used in these ways:

- A file associated with some HTML such as `about.html` or `about.php` or a view generated by a framework like `/about`.
- It can be a screen the user sees.

In most mobile frameworks you have what's called a multiple-page template. These templates allow your mobile application's HTML, PHP, or other files to serve multiple screens as viewed from the perspective of the user, all being contained within a master page and rendered via Ajax. This gives you the ability to have nice transitions between user-viewed pages, rather than the refreshes you typically experience on normal web sites.

More Data-Roles

From within the `data-role="page"`, you have three other data roles.

- `Data-role="header"` – This is the section of the document used as the page header.
- `Data-role="content"` – This is the section of the document used as the page content area.
- `Data-role="footer"` – This is the section of the document used as the page footer.

■ **Note** These do not correspond to the associated new elements such as `<header>`, `<footer>`, and `<section>` in HTML5. Rather these are element-level attributes and can be interchanged with the `<div>` tags specified on the demo web site.

When you put these together you end up with the sample page shown in Figure 5-1.

Figure 5-1. Sample page

So just as before, this page is rather simple and plain; the markup for this page is as follows.

Companion Site Reference

Example 5-3: Follow the link below to run this example on the companion site.

`http://www.learnhtml5book.com/chapter5/jquerymobile/headers.html`

```
<!doctype html>
<html>
<head>
    <meta charset="utf-8">
    <title>JQuery Mobile</title>
```

```
    <meta name="viewport" content="width=device-width" />
    <link rel="stylesheet" href="jquery.mobile-1.0b3.min.css" />
    <script src="jquery-1.6.4.min.js"></script>
    <script src="jquery.mobile-1.0b3.min.js"></script>
</head>
<body>
<div data-role="page">
  <header data-role="header">
    <h1>Page Title</h1>
  </header>
  <section data-role="content">
    <p>Page content goes here.</p>
  </section>
  <footer data-role="footer">
    <h4>Page Footer</h4>
  </footer>
</div>
</body>
</html>
```

Multipage Templates

This is a single page with multiple sections where content is shown. In reality it's just a hidden element that gets unhidden and moved around via a CSS transition, but to the user it looks like a new page or screen.

Companion Site Reference

Example 5-4: Follow the link below to run this example on the companion site.

`http://www.learnhtml5book.com/chapter5/jquerymobile/twopage.html`

```
<div data-role="page" id="one" data-title="page one">
  <header data-role="header">
    <h1>Page Title</h1>
  </header>
  <section data-role="content">
    <p>Page 1</p>
    <p><a href="#two">To Page 2</a></p>
  </section>
  <footer data-role="footer">
    <h4>Page Footer</h4>
  </footer>
</div>
<div data-role="page" id="two" data-title="page two">
  <header data-role="header">
    <h1>Page Title</h1>
  </header>
```

```
    <section data-role="content">
      <p>Page 2</p>
      <p><a href="#one">To Page 1</a></p>
    </section>
    <footer data-role="footer">
      <h4>Page Footer</h4>
    </footer>
</div>
```

You can see that moving between pages or screens all within the same file is rather easy. By default, your pages will all have the same `<title>`. To avoid this, use an element called `data-title`, as shown in the example above.

Linking to Other Pages/Files

Normally you would just need to set your page/file name in the `href` attribute of your `<a>` tag. But in jQuery mobile this behavior is overridden or Hijaxed and converted to an Ajax request. So `<a href="newpage.html">` actually makes an Ajax call to retrieve the page, and then it's loaded into the DOM.

To disable this behavior you can add one of these two attributes to your element:

`Rel="external"`

or

`data-ajax="false"`

You would want to use this if you're linking to a page with multiple internal pages such as a multipage template.

Moving Back

To move back to a previous page you just need to create a link with the attribute `data-rel="back"`.
We talk more about the back button later when we discuss buttons.

Page Transitions

Unlike traditional page transitions, where your page jumps to a new set of contents, with jQuery Mobile you have six different page transitions or effects. These are created via the element attribute called `data-transition`.

- Slide (default) – Causes the new page to slide in from the left
- Slideup – Causes new pages to slide in from the top
- Slidedown – Causes new pages to slide in from the bottom
- Pop – Causes new pages to pop in
- Fade – Causes new pages to fade in
- Flip – Causes new pages to flip in

You can also change the direction of the page transition by adding the attribute `data-direction="reverse"`.

Dialogs

Sometimes you don't want to take the user to a new page. You want the context and focus of the user to be on the current page, but you need to display new information relevant to a user action. For these you use dialogs.

To use a dialog instead of a page just add the element `data-rel="dialog"` to your `<a>` tag. The same transitions apply to how the dialog will appear as they do for page transitions.

To close the dialog just use the same `data-rel="back"` attribute we used for back button links. Again, we talk about using a nicer close button when we talk about buttons.

Scripting Pages

jQuery Mobile has the following mechanism for prefetching pages.

```
$.mobile.loadPage(pageurl);
```

▓ **Note** Be careful when continuously appending and adding to the page DOM. This has to do with the memory of your iOS device and the more pages loaded into memory the slower your mobile app will run.

For changing pages, use

```
$.mobile.changePage(to, transition, back, changeHash)
```

The arguments are defined as

- to – The page to which you want to change
- transition – The transition effect you would like
- back – A Boolean where true is forward and false is back
- changeHash – A Boolean to whether you'd like the URL's hash to be updated on success

A simple example of an anchor calling JavaScript with a transition either in HTML or called from JavaScript.

```
<a href="about.html" data-transition="pop">About</a>
- or
<a href="javascript:toAbout()">About</a>
...
function toAbout() {
  $.mobile.changePage( "about.html", { transition: "pop"} );
}
```

Toolbars and Buttons

Toolbars are used usually in headers and footers of your application. There's more detail on footer and navbars in the next chapter but for now we can talk about the basics and how to configure the header.

Header Toolbars

The default header is created by the following markup.

```
<header data-role="header">
  <h1>Page Title</h1>
</header>
```

To add a few buttons to the header we just use the following convention with three attributes: data-icon="back", data-rel="back".

```
<div data-role="header" data-position="inline">
        <a  data-icon="back" data-rel="back" back-btn="true">Back</a>
        <h1>Header</h1>
        <a href="index.html" data-icon="check">Save</a>
</div>
```

This gives you a button called "Save" and a functioning "Back Button" for your mobile app.

Figure 5-2. Header bar with buttons

Creating Buttons

From the previous example you saw that making a back button and a save button was nothing more than using the data-icon attribute. See Figure 5-2.

To make a normal <a> tag a button, use the data-role attribute.

Companion Site Reference

Example 5-5: Follow the link below to run this example on the companion site.

```
http://www.learnhtml5book.com/chapter5/jquerymobile/buttons.html
```

```
<a data-role="button">button text</a>
```

Or use normal form elements.

```
<button>button</button>
<input type="button" value="button">
<input type="submit" value="button">
<input type="image" src="img.jpg">
```

Button Icons

Button icons are all derived from an image in the jQuery Mobile download and have names such as arrow-r, gear, grid, star, and the like. You can review all of these from the jQuery Mobile site.

You can position the icon via the attribute: data-iconpos="right|top|bottom|notext". If you don't want text on the button you just need to specify notext instead of a position.

If you want your button to be compact just use the data-inline="true" attribute.

If you want to group your buttons, wrap all your buttons in an element with the attribute: data-role="controlgroup".

You can view a few examples of these attributes in Figure 5-3.

Figure 5-3. Button examples

The full code for Figure 5-3 is shown below.

```
<section data-role="content">
  <p><a href="index.html" data-role="button" data-icon="home">Normal</a></p>
  <p><a href="index.html" data-role="button" data-inline="true">Compact</a></p>
  <div data-role="controlgroup" data-type="horizontal">
      <a href="index.html" data-role="button">A</a>
      <a href="index.html" data-role="button">B</a>
      <a href="index.html" data-role="button">C</a>
  </div>
</section>
```

List Views

All lists on jQuery Mobile take the form of the <ul> and <li> tags with the attribute data-role="listview"
for the <ul> tag.

There are several ways to create lists with jQuery Mobile. In some of the examples shown in Figure 5-4 you can include: Basic List, List with Counts, and List with Thumbnails. You need to decide which list is best for you and it all depends on how much information you want or need to show.

In the mobile app in the Putting It All Together section I use all three list types, but not all of them in the same context. Be consistent but also try to remain flexible as you design your pages.

Companion Site Reference

Example 5-6: Follow the link below to run this example on the companion site.

```
http://www.learnhtml5book.com/chapter5/jquerymobile/lists.html
```

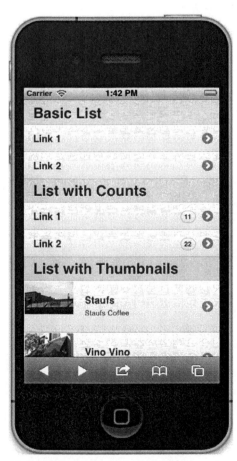

Figure 5-4. Basic and count lists

Here is the full HTML markup for the examples shown in Figure 5-4.

```
<h1>Basic List</h1>
    <ul data-role="listview">
        <li><a href="">Link 1</a></li>
        <li><a href="">Link 2</a></li>
    </ul>
<h1>List with Counts</h1>
<ul data-role="listview">
        <li><a href="">Link 1</a><span class="ui-li-count ui-btn-up-c ui-btn-↵
corner-all">11</span></li>
        <li><a href="">Link 2</a><span class="ui-li-count ui-btn-up-c ui-btn-↵
corner-all">22</span></li>
  </ul>
<h1>List with Thumbnails</h1>
        <ul data-role="listview">
        <li><a href="index.html" class="ui-link-inherit">
        <img src="staufs_thumb.jpg" class="ui-li-thumb">
        <h3 class="ui-li-heading">Staufs</h3>
        <p class="ui-li-desc">Staufs Coffee</p>
        </a>
        </li>
        <li><a href="index.html" class="ui-link-inherit">
          <img src="vino-vino_thumb.jpg" class="ui-li-thumb">
          <h3 class="ui-li-heading">Vino Vino</h3>
          <p class="ui-li-desc">Vino Vino Restaurant</p>
            </a>
        </li>
    </ul>
```

■ **Note** Keep in mind that showing a lot of information on a long list can cause a performance hit.

A Short Note on Themes

One thing I've not mentioned yet are the different themes offered with jQuery Mobile. There are five themes:

- **Theme A** (default) – Black and dark grey background and white text
- **Theme B** – Blue background and white text
- **Theme C** – Light gray background with black text
- **Theme D** – White background with black text
- **Theme E** – Yellow background with black text

To use any of these themes just apply the data-theme attribute to pages, toolbars, content, buttons, and list as in:

```
<header data-role="header" data-theme="b">
```

▓ **Note** Soon jQuery Mobile will have a custom theme roller similar to jQuery UI that will allow you to create your own themes and use them on your mobile site.

Putting It All Together

Now that we have our mobile framework we're ready to create the home page of GrandviewAve.com mobile edition.

First we'll need to add our jQuery mobile JS and CSS files to the header.

```
<head>
    <title>Welcome To Grandview Ave.</title>
    <meta name="viewport" content="width=device-width" />
    <link rel="stylesheet" href="css/jquery.mobile-1.0b3.min.css" />
    <link rel="stylesheet" href="css/grandviewave.css" />
    <script src="js/jquery-1.6.2.min.js"></script>
    <script src="js/jquery.mobile-1.0b3.min.js"></script>
```

Next we need to load the content from the API for the business categories.

```
<script type="text/javascript">
$().ready(function(){
    $.mobile.pageLoading();
    $.get('api/cats.php', function(data) {
        $('#cats').html(data);
        $('#cats ul').listview();
        $.mobile.pageLoading(true);
    });
    preload();
});
    function preload() {
<?php
for ($i=0;$i<7;$i++) {
?>
        $.get('api/profiles.php?id=<?=$i?>', function(data) {
            $('#list_<?=$i?>').html(data);
            $('#cat_<?=$i?>').page();
        });
<? }?>
    }
</script>
</head>
```

Note that I used a little PHP in this file. I did this to build the loop of preloaded profile list dynamically into the DOM. I could have hard-coded it but my file would be rather large.

Next we create the first mobile "page". This will be the home page as seen by users.

```
<div data-role="page">
  <header data-role="header">
    <div class="header1">
        <img src="images/logo.png" alt="welcome to grandviewave.com">
    </div>
```

```
    </header>
    <section data-role="content">
       <div id="cats"></div>
    </section>
</div>
```

Finally we create the subsequent pages, again using a little PHP:

```
<?
for ($i=0;$i<7;$i++) {
?>
<div data-role="page" id="cat_<?=$i?>">
    <header data-role="header">
      <a data-icon="back" data-rel="back" back-btn="true">Back</a>
      <div class="header2">
        <img src="images/logo.png" alt="gave.com"/>
      </div>
    </header>
    <div data-role="content">
        <div id="list_<?=$i?>"></div>
    </div>
</div>
<? }?>
```

The API side of this call looks like this:

```
<ul data-role="listview" data-inset="true" data-theme="c" data-dividertheme="a">
<li data-role="list-divider">Business Directory</li>
<li><a href="#cat_0">All</a></li>
<? foreach ($cats as $cat) { ?>
<li><a href="#cat_<?=$cat->id?>"><?=$cat->name?></a></li>
<? } ?>
</ul>
```

You might notice that we're not using JSON at this time because that makes the page a little more complicated and the data set is not that large.

Figure 5-5 shows a simple home page made by creating and decorating a list of business categories. This takes you to a more detailed list of businesses.

Figure 5-5. *Grandview Ave home page*

This is followed by the next page with a smaller logo, back button, and a list with icons (Figure 5-6).

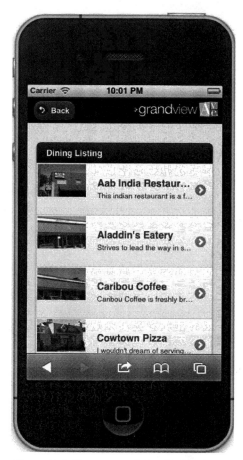

Figure 5-6. Next page of detailed listings

The site is already taking shape. But notice that although we are using the mobile framework for controlling our pages and getting the information dynamically, there are still some things that are missing.

- Fixed tabbed navigation to navigate between all the pages of the site
- Touch events such as scrolling and swiping
- No mention of design for the iPad

Summary

This chapter talked about using the jQuery Mobile framework rather than creating all the CSS and JS yourself. We used some of concepts from the previous chapters but due to the conventions and the out-of-the-box functionality we didn't need to do much.

Before moving on to the next chapter you should know how to:

- Create a basic jQuery mobile page.

- Create a multipage template.

- Add dynamic content to your pages via AJAX.

- Create headers and buttons with various themes.

These items above give us a great start to completing our mobile web application, however, there are still a few pieces missing, mainly revolving around navigation, touch interactions, and how to take advantage of the extra screen real estate with the iPad. That's what I talk about next.

CHAPTER 6

Usability, Navigation, and Touch

This is the chapter where I focus on how your user will interact with your mobile site. It's the glue that holds everything else together. Because you're designing for a mobile site and not a native app, you need to keep in mind the usage paradigm for your users has been affected not by websites, but by native apps. So this means they'll want to interact with your mobile site in the same way they do with their favorite apps.

Another thing you need to decide is whether you want to be orientation sensitive. You need to ask the question: does your navigation change based on whether you're in landscape or portrait mode?

Of course this begs a larger question. How do users interact with your mobile site? Or what do you want the user experience (UX) to be like for your site? How do you want users to navigate, or use touch interaction?

I talk about a little of everything starting with user experience or usability.

Usability

What's usability? Basically it's the ease of use and learnability of a system, in our case a mobile website built with HTML5 and JavaScript. Much has been done to enhance user experience in the past five years with technologies such as Ajax, user-centered design, and page-as-an application metaphors. In fact I would say user experience is probably the best it's ever been, but that translates differently to the iPhone and iPad because you have the following additional constraints.

- Small screen size
- Smaller memory
- Slower performance
- Slower download
- Awkward input

Sometimes constraints are good because they cause you to focus on the essentials; other times they make things downright difficult to work. Here are some tips to help you out.

Small Form Factor Tips

The following are some things to think about when programming for 320 pixels versus 1,024 or larger.

- *Limit Content to the Essential:* Because you can focus your target users on exactly what they need.

- *Limit Navigation Areas:* Because you might have less content to navigate to and from, creating a small flat navigation will allow users to get to the content on your site fast.

- *Limit the Physical Size of Content:* Because using large images or lots of text requiring scrolling will make your user's fingers get tired.

Performance Tips

The following are some things to think about when your user has a slower network connection and slower processor.

- *Minify your CSS and JS:* Because this will allow your site to download faster and appear as snappy as a native app. See Chapter 3 (`mod_deflate`).

- *Optimize away from frameworks or plugins:* Because as your app gets more sophisticated lightening up the script and HTML footprint of your site/app has a surprising effect on performance.

- *Prefetch and cache content locally:* Because this will allow your site to download everything on first load as opposed to loading it as you go.

Input Tips

Here are some things to think about when users don't have a keyboard.

- Limit forms and text searches because keyboards are a little awkward on touch devices; having large forms or requiring search is probably not a good thing.

- Use custom form widgets from HTML5.

- Use custom buttons from jQuery Mobile.

- Try to use swipe or other touch gestures for navigation versus having users hunt for navigation.

Other Tips

Finally, the following are just a few other usability tips you might try as you develop your site.

- If you use Ajax or jQuery Mobile to load your pages, make sure to use a loading image to show that the system is working.

- Try to use common places in the header or footer for things such as settings or home icons.

- Don't try to reinvent the mobile paradigm. Users are accustomed to using mobile apps in a certain way; if they have to think, then you're going to make your site less usable.

- Link your images.

- Put your app in front of your parents or kids and then ask them to use it without giving them any instructions.

Site Navigation

A natural byproduct of making your mobile site usable is to make it easy to navigate. So for that I'll now talk about some common navigation design patterns.

- *Tree Drill Down:* This is where you take a large collection of data, classify it, and refine what you're looking for as you drill down, usually in the form of a list.

- *Header Menus:* This is where you provide tabs, buttons, or tools in the header to assist in navigation.

- *Footers and Tab Bars:* This is where you provide tabs for your user to move horizontally across your site rather than having to use the back button to move back to the home page in order to drill back down to another area of the site.

- *Overlays and Modals:* This is where instead of navigating to a page you just provide an overlay of information. This is useful when you don't want the user to lose context but the information is not sufficient for an entire page.

All of these types of navigation are supported by jQuery Mobile. Let's look at them in more detail.

Tree Drill-Down and Headers

This kind of navigation works best if you are filtering through information that's naturally organized and grouped. To use this kind of navigation, just create a list view and link it.

In Figure 6-1, the right image has a back button which is in the header providing easy navigation to the previous page.

Companion Site Reference

Examples 6-1 and 6-2: Follow the links below to run these examples on the companion site.

```
http://www.learnhtml5book.com/chapter6/drill1.php
http://www.learnhtml5book.com/chapter6/drill2.php
```

Figure 6-1. Tree Drill-Down

The source code for this example is insanely easy:

```
<ul data-role="listview">
    <li><a href="drill2.html">Link 1</a></li>
    <li><a href="drill2.html">Link 2</a></li>
</ul>
```

And for the second page, I just added a back button:

```
<header data-role="header" data-theme="b">
<a data-icon="back" data-add-back-btn="true" data-rel="back">Back</a>
<h1>Drill Page 2</h1>
</header>
<section data-role="content">
<h1>Drill Down List</h1>
<ul data-role="listview">
    <li><a href="drill3.html">More 1</a></li>
    <li><a href="drill3.html">More 2</a></li>
</ul>
</section>
```

Tabbed Navigation

You can add tabs to your site in a few ways. Top tabs can be designed very similarly to traditional web navigation with a top navigation.

Bottom navigation can be a little more complicated in that sometimes you might want to fix the navigation at the bottom so it looks like a native tab bar. Fortunately with iOS5, you can specify a scroll size and fix your navigation as opposed to having to do JavaScript to move your navigation as you scroll, although I've not shown that in this chapter.

This kind of navigation works best if you have a limited number of areas you want to take your user, usually five or less, where you can then apply other navigation styles from within a tab.

In Figure 6-2, I've created a two-tab footer navigation. Note the styles and that the buttons are evenly spaced. This is done automatically by jQuery Mobile, saving you from having to space them or alternate CSS based on orientation changes.

jQuery also provides image icons for these images to make them appear very close to the iOS tab bar design pattern.

Companion Site Reference

Example 6-3: Follow the link below to run this example on the companion site.

```
http://www.learnhtml5book.com/chapter6/tabs.php
```

Figure 6-2. *Tab bar from Native iOS App*

Again the code for this is really easy with jQuery Mobile. I just added the following attributes to the footer, data-role, data-position="fixed", then created another data-role called navbar with some more list.

The colors and states are maintained through convention via the class names ui-btn-active and ui-state-persist.

```
<footer data-role="footer" data-position="fixed">
<div data-role="navbar">
<ul>
    <li><a href="drill1.html" class="ui-btn-active ui-state-persist"↵
    data-transition="fade">one</a></li>
    <li><a href="drill2.html" class="ui-state-persist" data-transition="fade">two</a></li>
</ul>
</div>
</footer>
```

Dialogs and Modals

With jQuery Mobile creating a dialog is as simple as adding the attribute `data-rel="dialog"` to your `<a>` or `<button>`. Then when you click the (X) of the dialog you will be taken back to your original page.

Companion Site Reference

Example 6-4: Follow the link below to run this example on the companion site.

`http://www.learnhtml5book.com/chapter6/modals.php`

I have some simple content in the screenshot shown in Figure 6-3.

Figure 6-3. Sample Dialog Window

Simple content is the best for dialogs as you don't want them to be larger than two-thirds of the screen. Although the example above is plain, usually it's overlaying a page of information or providing other functionality to support the underlying page.

Navigating for the iPad

I wanted to talk a little bit about how you would use your current framework with the iPad. In general you have three options:

- *Option 1.* Modify your current site to be iPad-compatible. This can be little or no work, but if your site is optimized for a mouse it might not work that well for touch interaction.

- *Option 2.* Modify your mobile navigation for the iPad. This should work out of the box, but it will look strange on a larger surface.

- *Option 3.* Create a completely new site just for the iPad. You can have a lot of additional work and some mobile frameworks are not optimized for tablet interfaces.

In the example below I've hacked together a little jQuery Mobile, and although it works, it's not as nice an experience as the native site. Good thing I talked about how to roll your own CSS and JS in the previous chapters because Option 3 will require you do just that.

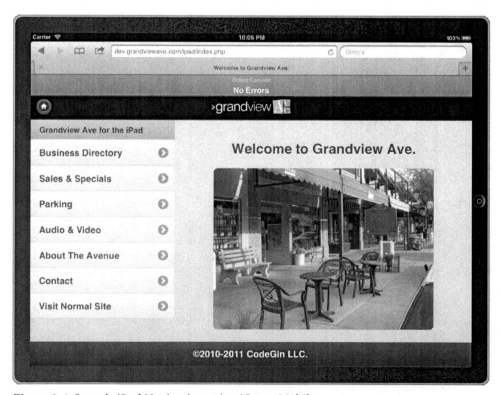

Figure 6-4. Sample iPad Navigation using jQuery Mobile

iPad Tips

- jQuery Mobile does not work too well with iPad, so although this mobile framework works great for your iPod Touch or iPhone, you will find it lacking in several areas for the iPad.

- You have some more area, so your content will need to scale to this area. One way is to use the navigation metaphor pictured in Figure 6-4 and combine the landscape mode of your iPhone project for body content on the right.

- You can make better use of the toolbar not only because it's longer but because you can have more icons and even a menu on the right to drop down and provide context.

- On an OrientationChange event, hide the navigation so that your body content remains roughly the same size.

- You might have better performance on the iPad because most usage will be without 3G and over WiFi. So think about where users will be using their iPad when considering performance and content size.

Working with a Larger Body Area

With the iPad you have roughly 65% of 1,024 pixels or just over 650 px of body area. This content size might roughly equate to the same area you're using on your normal website.

So rather than starting from your mobile content, I'd suggest that you just use what content you have on your main site. You can then adapt the content by adding some iPad navigation features.

Creating a Header

The header was very similar to the iPhone version as you can see below.

```
<header data-role="header">
    <a data-icon="home" href="/ipad/index.php" data-iconpos="notext">Home</a>
        <div class="header2">
            <a href="/m" rel="external"><img src="/m/images/logo.png" alt="welcome to↵
grandviewave.com" border="0"></a>
        </div>
    </header>
```

Creating a Left Nav

The very first thing I did was create a container and float it to the left. Next I changed the navigation a little so that it was continued by jQuery Mobile and such that I changed the theme to the selected page to a different theme so that it stood out.

▓ **Note** The PHP in the page does nothing more than check for the name of the page so that it can modify the style. There are many ways to do this but I thought I'd just show you something rather simple and easy to follow.

```
<div style="width:30%;float:left;">
    <ul data-role="listview" data-theme="c" data-dividertheme="d">
        <li data-role="list-divider">Grandview Ave for the iPad</li>
        <li <? if (PAGE_NAME == "/ipad/directory.php") echo 'data-theme="a"';?>>
        <a href="directory.php" data-transition="fade" class=↵
"ui-state-persist">Business Directory</a></li>
        <li <? if (PAGE_NAME == "/ipad/sales.php") echo 'data-theme="a"';?>>
        <a href="sales.php" data-transition="fade" class=↵
"ui-state-persist">Sales &amp; Specials</a></li>
        <li <? if (PAGE_NAME == "/ipad/parking.php") echo 'data-theme="a"';?>>
        <a href="parking.php" data-transition="fade" class=↵
"ui-state-persist">Parking</a></li>
        <li <? if (PAGE_NAME == "/ipad/audvid.php") echo 'data-theme="a"';?>>
        <a href="audvid.php" data-transition="fade" class=↵
"ui-state-persist">Audio &amp; Video</a></li>
        <li <? if (PAGE_NAME == "/ipad/about.php") echo 'data-theme="a"';?>>
        <a href="about.php" data-transition="fade" class=↵
"ui-state-persist">About The Avenue</a></li>
        <li <? if (PAGE_NAME == "/ipad/contact.php") echo 'data-theme="a"';?>>
        <a href="contact.php" data-transition="fade" class=↵
"ui-state-persist">Contact</a></li>
        <li><a href="/" rel="external">Visit Normal Site</a></li>
    </ul>
</div>
```

For the right part (or body) of the page I again just wrapped it in a <div> and floated it right.

```
<div style="width:65%;float:left;margin-left:35px;">
    <h1 style="text-align:center;">Some Title<h1>
</div>
```

Creating a Footer

Again, as with the header I was able to create a footer in much the same way as I did with the iPhone.

```
<div data-role="footer" data-position="fixed">
    <h1>&copy;2010-2012 CodeGin LLC.</h1>
</div>
```

Touch Interactions

So although the constraints presented earlier make programming your site a little more difficult there's something you get with iOS devices you don't readily get from the computer, and that's touch interactions. Touch interactions, if done correctly, can really improve the usability of your site.

One-Finger Events

These events just require a single finger and can be used to tap (vs. click), swipe left or right, or scroll up or down.

- *Tap:* Just like a single click.

- *Double Tap:* Just a like a double click.
- *Swipe (Left, Right, Up, Down):* Tap then drag your finger in a certain direction.

Multitouch Events

These events happen when two or more fingers are used to interact with the surface of your iPhone or iPad.

- *Pinch:* Usually to zoom out in the case of a larger website or Google map
- *Spread:* Usually to zoom in in the case of a nonviewport website or Google map
- *Rotate:* To rotate an object clockwise or counterclockwise

Supported Events by Mobile Safari

- TouchStart: Happens every time a finger is placed on the surface.
- TouchEnd: Happens every time a finger is removed from the surface.
- TouchMove: Happens when a finger is on a surface and is moved.
- TouchCancel: Not really a practical event, but this is when the system cancels the tracking for a touch.
- GestureStart: When two or more fingers touch the surface.
- GestureEnd: When the gesture ends or just one or no more fingers are touching the surface.
- GestureChange: When both fingers move while touching the surface.

An example of coding your own swipe left or swipe right gesture events would look something like this.

Companion Site Reference

Examples 6-5: Follow the link below to run this example on the companion site.

`http://www.learnhtml5book.com/chapter6/events.php`

```
<div data-role="page">
<header data-role="header" data-theme="b">
<h1>Touch Example</h1>
</header>
<div id="testarea" style="width:200px;height:200px;background:#ccc;"></div>
</div>
<script type="text/javascript">

    var box = document.querySelector("#testarea");
    var startX = 0;
```

```
    var startY = 0;
    var endX = 0;
    var endY = 0;

    box.ontouchstart=function(evt){
      startX = evt.pageX;
      startY = evt.pageY;
    }

    box.ontouchend=function(evt){
      var endX = evt.changedTouches[0].pageX;
      var delta = (startX-endX);
      var deltaY = Math.abs(startY - endY);
      endY = evt.pageY;
      if (delta > 40 && endX > 0 && startX > 0 && deltaY < 20) {
          alert ("left swipe")
      }
      if (delta < -40 && endX > 0 && startX > 0 && deltaY < 20) {
          alert ("right swipe")
      }
      startX=0;
      endX=0;
      startX = 0;
      startY = 0;
    }
```

</script>

By measuring the pageX at the start and end of the event, you can calculate whether the finger was swiped to the left or to the right with a little math. But you don't need to work this out yourself: jQuery Mobile has it built in.

jQuery Mobile Events

Underneath the covers of jQuery Mobile these events encapsulate touch- and click-related events.

- Tap: After a complete touch event.

- Taphold: Touching the screen for about a second.

- Swipe: Triggers when there's a drag of more than 30 px within a one-second duration.

- Swipeleft: Triggers when a swipe is done in the left direction.

- Swiperight: Triggers when a swipe is done in the right direction.

- ScrollStart: Triggers when an item is scrolled up or down.

- ScrollStop: Triggers when the scroll stops.

Below I show you how to execute the gestures via some JavaScript. The swipe event will always fire in the case of swipeleft and swiperight.

The tap event will also be fired if you just touch the screen and will always fire before the taphold event. So comment out the ones you don't want to use.

Companion Site Reference

Example 6-6: Follow the link below to run this example on the companion site.

http://www.learnhtml5book.com/chapter6/events2.php

```
<script type="text/javascript">
      $('body').live('swipe', function(e) {
          alert('You swiped!');
          e.stopImmediatePropagation();
          return false;
      });
      $('body').live('swipeleft', function(e) {
          alert('You swiped left!');
          e.stopImmediatePropagation();
          return false;
      });
      $('body').live('swiperight', function(e) {
          alert('You swiped right!');
          e.stopImmediatePropagation();
          return false;
      });
      $('body').live('tap', function(e) {
          alert('You tapped!');
          e.stopImmediatePropagation();
          return false;
      });
      $('body').live('taphold', function(e) {
          alert('You are touching the screen!');
          e.stopImmediatePropagation();
          return false;
      });

</script>
```

Putting It All Together

So far for GrandviewAve we've just built a basic directory structure. Now it's time to link these files together into a cohesive navigation. I use a combination of navigation metaphors for the site: drill-down, a tab bar footer, and a header with some buttons.

The drill-down allows users to navigate the business directory by category and the tabbed footer allows users to move to different parts of the site without having to go back home.

I didn't know quite how I wanted to do it, so let me show you some of the options I created during the design.

Option 1

The first option I thought about was a plain list (Figure 6-5). This did everything I needed it to do: display a list of the navigational areas and allow users to drill down to everything all the way to the individual business.

But this didn't quite have the kind of usability I wanted because every time I would need to look for parking or find out sales and specials I'd have to go back or click the top logo.

Figure 6-5. Nav Drill Down (Option #1)

Option 2

The second option (Figure 6-6) was a bit closer mainly because of the footer navigation. This navigation allowed me to jump between businesses and parking.

But like Option 1 it was still a little plain.

Figure 6-6. *Footer Tabbed Navigation (Option 2)*

Option 3

With Option 2 I had all the navigation elements I wanted users to access in the footer, except for the directory. So I just added the business directory to the home page via a single link and the rest of the application could now be accessed via the footer.

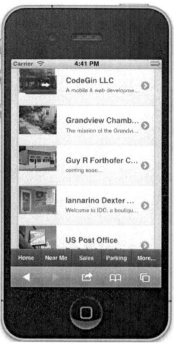

Figure 6-7. Combined Footer & Drill-down (Final)

In Figure 6-7 the left screen is the home page, the middle one is the business directory drill-down, followed by a business detail page, in this case Iannarino Dexter Creative.

To explain the code for each let's start with the header. There are two: one for the home page and the second with the back button and home icon. The class names `header1` and `header2` just define some of the parameters such as the background and size of the logo. You can ignore them as they contain no conventional aspects.

Header 1—Home Page

This is just a plain vanilla header with the attribute `data-role="header"`.

```
<header data-role="header">
<div class="header1">
<a href="/m/index.php" rel="external"><img src="images/logo.png" alt="welcome to↩
 grandviewave.com" border="0"></a>
</div>
</header>
```

Header 2—Subsequent Pages

This is slightly different because we have two buttons: one the back button specified by an `<a>` tag with `data-add-back-btn`, `data-rel`, and `data-icon` attributes, and the second with another `<a>` tag for the home icon with the `data-iconpos="notext"` attribute specifying no text.

```
<header data-role="header">
<a data-icon="back" data-add-back-btn="true" data-rel="back">Back</a>
<div class="header2">
<a href="/m" rel="external"><img src="images/logo.png" alt="welcome to↵
 grandviewave.com" border="0"></a>
</div>
<a data-icon="home" href="#home" data-iconpos="notext">Home</a>
</header>
```

The combination of these two headers is used in the entire mobile site and swapped out dynamically on the pages via some crude PHP:

```
<? if ($_SERVER['SCRIPT_NAME'] == "/m/index.php") {?>.
```

Footer Navigation

The second part of the navigation is what's in the footer. First it's sticky to the bottom of the page via the two attributes data-role="footer" and data-position="fixed".

The colors are added via the class names: ui-btn-activeui-state-persist, and the fade transition is created via the attribute: data-transition="fade".

I chose the fade transition because it seemed to look a little better on my iPhone than the "slide" transition that's there by default. I seemed to get a shrinking flash effect that just seemed a little odd.

```
<div data-role="footer" data-position="fixed">
<div data-role="navbar">
<ul>
        <li><a href="/m/index.php" class="ui-btn-active ui-state-persist"↵
        data-transition="fade">Home</a></li>
        <li><a href="/m/near.php" class=" ui-state-persist"↵
        data-transition="fade">Near Me</a></li>
        <li><a href="/m/sales.php" class=" ui-state-persist"↵
        data-transition="fade">Sales</a></li>
        <li><a href="/m/parking.php" class=" ui-state-persist"↵
        data-transition="fade">Parking</a></li>
        <li><a href="/m/more.php" class=" ui-state-persist"↵
        data-transition="fade">More</a></li>
</ul>
</div>
</div></div>
```

So far I've not had the need for any touch effects so I'm not going to add any of those at this time.

Chapter Summary

This chapter combined all the pieces and parts we've discussed up until now and put it all together into a usable navigation and talked about how to add touch events to your mobile web app.

Before moving on to the next chapter you should know how to do the following.

- Understand the constraints of building a mobile web app compared with a desktop web app.

- Understand the main mobile navigation patterns: drill-down, header, footer, and modal windows.

- How to use touch interactions on your mobile web app.

- How to use jQuery Mobile to navigate, transition, and glue your site together.

Next I begin filling in some of the content areas of the Grandview Ave web app such as Parking, Near Me functionality, and business locations.

CHAPTER 7

GPS and Google Maps

Of all the mobile web development I've done, I've had the most fun working with the Global Positioning System (GPS). GPS gives you as the developer a lot of power to connect the real world to a web site or mobile app that provides a connection to your user that is far more intimate than technologies such as user preferences or personalization.

To make things even better, what if you had the entire world that could be viewed through either road maps or satellite photos and everything could be interfaced via JavaScript? Hey, we have something for that, and it's called Google Maps.

The one thing about having both of these at your disposal is you can add incredibly powerful functionality with very little code.

Getting GPS Coordinates

GPS coordinates are measured with longitude and latitude.

- *Longitude*: The vertical lines on the globe. The longitude of 0.0 is the Prime Meridian and runs through Greenwich, England. Changes in longitude often correspond to time zone changes. When you move east, the longitude goes +, or east, and if you go west of Greenwich, longitude goes –, or west. For example, Columbus, Ohio, would be -83 (or 83 west), and Seattle, Washington, would be -122 (or 122 west).

- A degree of longitude is approximately 69 miles at the equator, but gradually goes to zero as you move closer to a pole. So, if you're on the equator and drive 69 miles east, you'll be at longitude 1 degree east.

- *Latitude*: The horizontal lines on the globe. The latitude of 0.0 degrees is the equator. Changes in latitude would be how far north or how far south of the equator you move, where 90 is the North Pole and -90 is the South Pole. The latitude of 39 would be Columbus, Ohio (or 39 north).

- A degree of latitude is approximately 69 miles. So, once again, if you're at the equator and drive 69 miles north, your latitude would be 1 degree north. Furthermore, a *minute*, or 1/60th of a degree, is approximately 1.15 miles, and a *second* of latitude is 1/3600th of a degree or just over 100 feet.

The GPS function that's built into iOS is the `navigator.geolocation` object. There are two methods for getting the GPS:

- `getCurrentPosition`: This will get the GPS position once.
- `watchCurrentPosition`: This will get the GPS position on a timed interval.

Companion Site Reference

Example 7-1: Follow the link below to run this example on the companion site.

http://www.learnhtml5book.com/chapter7/basics.php.

Both of these methods take as parameters a success function, an error function, and options in the form of JSON syntax. In the following example, I just create a button that calls the getGPS function that invokes the navigator.geolocation.getPosition method (see Figure 7-1).

■ **Note** The enableHighAccuracy option provides you with the highest accuracy. However, this option as well as watchCurrentPosition will consume a lot of battery life because GPS is a high-power activity.

```
<script>
function getGPS(){
    navigator.geolocation.getCurrentPosition(successGPS, errorGPS,↵
 {enableHighAccuracy : true});
}
function successGPS(position) {
    var lat = position.coords.latitude;
    var lon = position.coords.longitude;
    var curHTML = $('#gps_coords').html() + "lat="+lat + ",lon="+lon+"<br>";
    $('#gps_coords').html(curHTML);
}

function errorGPS() {
    alert('GPS Error');
}
</script>
<button onclick="getGPS()">Get GPS Coordinates</button>
<h2>GPS Coords Below</h2>
<div id="gps_coords"></div>
```

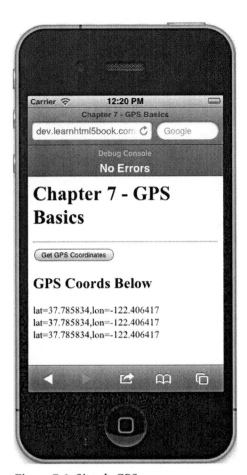

Figure 7-1. Simple GPS app

If you want to poll the GPS coordinates or get continuous feedback, you can use the watchPosition method. This returns the GPS coordinates to your callback function approximately once per second.

```
var updateLocation;

function watchGPS() {
  updateLocation = navigator.geolocation.watchPosition(
    successGPS, errorGPS,{enableHighAccuracy : true});
}

function clearWatch() {
  navigator.geolocation.clearWatch(updateLocation);
}
```

Using Google Maps

The Google Maps API gives you the ability to interact with road and satellite maps accessible via Google and use Google Maps on your mobile site; all you need are a few lines of code.

A Simple Map Example

In this simple example, we reference the Google Maps JavaScript file from Google and then create an `initialize()` function. This function name is just arbitrary; it can be anything you want. It either can be initialized via `body.onload` or via jQuery in `$().ready` or can be initialized manually via some button click or other kind of event.

The first thing you do is create a `LatLng` object with a latitude and longitude in the constructor followed by some options, specifically:

- `zoom`: This is the zoom scale of the map you are displaying.

- `center`: This is a `LatLng` object that centers your map.

- `mapTypeId`: This is whether you are displaying a `ROADMAP`, `HYBRID`, `SATELLITE`, or `TERRAIN`.

Finally, you just create a `Map` object, assigned to a variable for reference, with a constructor of an element from which it needs to reside. Based on the width and height of this element, the Google map will autosize and center.

Companion Site Reference

Example 7-2: Follow the link below to run this example on the companion site.

`http://www.learnhtml5book.com/chapter7/gmap.php`.

```
<script type="text/javascript" src="http://maps.googleapis.com/maps/↵
api/js?sensor=false">
</script>
<script type="text/javascript">
  function initialize() {
    var latlng = new google.maps.LatLng(39.985764, -83.044776);
    var myOptions = {
      zoom: 10,
      center: latlng,
      mapTypeId: google.maps.MapTypeId.ROADMAP
    };
    var map = new google.maps.Map(document.getElementById("basic_map"),
        myOptions);
  }
    $().ready(function(){
       initialize();
    });
</script>
<div id="basic_map" style="width:320px;height:240px;"></div>
```

Figure 7-2 shows the resulting page and map.

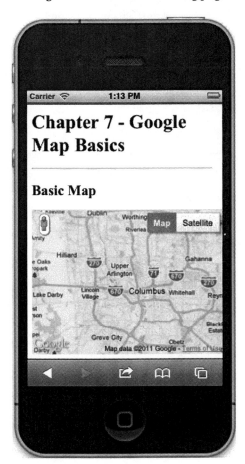

Figure 7-2. Simple Google Maps usage

Geocoding and Markers

Sometimes you don't have a longitude and latitude, so what do you do? Well, here's where something called *geocoding* comes into play. Geocoding is the process of finding a longitude and latitude via such data as street address and ZIP or postal codes.

The Google Geocoder class takes a GeocoderRequest object (JSON Address object) and returns a LatLng object.

To use this instead of the LatLng variable, just create the GeoCoder object, pass in a valid GeocoderRequest, and pass the resultant LatLng object to the initialize function.

It is also helpful to show the LatLng you're centering on. You do that with Google Maps via a Marker.

The Marker object takes as part of its constructor MarkerOptions (more JSON), and in the following example I've added two properties:

- position: The LatLng coordinate of the marker

- map: The Map object you're applying the marker

The following example shows you how to use both geocoding and a marker with a basic Google map. You can see the results in Figure 7-3.

Companion Site Reference

Example 7-3: Follow the link below to run this example on the companion site.

www.learnhtml5book.com/chapter7/gmap2.php.

```
<h2>Address Map</h2>
<script type="text/javascript" src="http://maps.googleapis.com/maps/
api/js?sensor=false">
</script>
<script type="text/javascript">
  function initialize(location) {
   var myOptions = {
      zoom: 17,
      center: location,
      mapTypeId: google.maps.MapTypeId.ROADMAP
   }
   var map = new google.maps.Map(document.getElementById("basic_map"), myOptions);
   var marker = new google.maps.Marker({
      position: location,
      map: map
   });
  }
    $().ready(function(){
      var geocoder = new google.maps.Geocoder();
      geocoder.geocode( { 'address': '1373 grandview ave. columbus ohio 43212'},
  function(results, status) {
          initialize(results[0].geometry.location);
      });
   });
</script>
<div id="basic_map" style="width:320px;height:240px;"></div>
```

Figure 7-3. *Simple geocoding example*

Static Maps

Sometimes you just need a picture of a map and might want to place markers on it. You can do this with Google Maps API v3, but you will have a lot of JavaScript, and it's performance-intensive for a phone, even if it's a dual- or quad-core iOS device.

For this Google has given you the ability to create a map via a URL that you can place as an image source.

Companion Site Reference

Example 7-4: Follow the link below to run this example on the companion site.

```
http://www.learnhtml5book.com/chapter7/static.php.
```

Static Google Map URL Pattern

Here's an example of the URL pattern and the parameters you might use when requesting a static Google map:

```
http://maps.googleapis.com/maps/api/staticmap?
```

Center

In this case, an address will automatically be geocoded to a latitude and longitude.

```
center=1373%20grandview%20ave,columbus,oh%2043212
```

Options

Here I'm setting the zoom level, size of the image, and type of map.

```
&zoom=14&size=320x240&maptype=roadmap
```

Marker

Finally, I set the color of the label, its text as *, and its location in latitude and longitude.

```
markers=color:red%7Ccolor:red%7Clabel:*%7C39.985764,-83.044776
```

Full Example

Here's the full example (Figure 7-4):

```
<img src="http://maps.googleapis.com/maps/api/staticmap?center=1373%20grandview%20ave,↵
columbus,oh%2043212&zoom=14&size=320x240&maptype=roadmap&markers=color:red%7Ccolor:↵
red%7Clabel:*%7C39.985764,-83.044776&sensor=false">
```

Figure 7-4. Simple static maps example

Interacting with Google Maps via GPS

So, you've been able to get GPS coordinates from your phone, and you've been able to create a few basic Google maps, but how do you connect the two?

First, you will be moving on a map, so you'll need a way to update your position on a map. Next, you will want to identify where you want to go. To designate those two places, use two markers.

The first marker will be a *blue dot* that will represent your current location. For the second marker you'll just use a standard red pin. For the blue dot, I've used a custom `MarkerImage` (`blue_dot.png` file). In Chapter 8, I'll use pure CSS.

After you create the markers, create the `initialize` function to take the coordinates of your position (a `LatLng` object) and place that marker created earlier to the position on your Google map.

When the page loads (implemented by JQuery `$.ready`), you can call `watchPosition`, which invokes the `successGPS` function. The `successGPS` function in turn creates a new marker with this location, which will show you your current location relative to your goal location (the red pin marker). If this occurs each second, you'll get a lot of markers if you don't reuse the variable name.

Companion Site Reference

Example 7-5: Follow the link below to run this example on the companion site.

www.learnhtml5book.com/chapter7/currentlocation.php.

```
<script type="text/javascript" src="http://maps.googleapis.com/maps/↵
api/js?sensor=false">
</script>

<h2>Current Location</h2>

<script type="text/javascript">
    var map;
    var bluedot = new google.maps.MarkerImage('blue_dot.png',
            new google.maps.Size(38, 38),
            new google.maps.Point(0, 0),
            new google.maps.Point(19, 19)
            );

    function initialize(location) {
        var myOptions = {
            zoom: 17,
            center: location,
            mapTypeId: google.maps.MapTypeId.ROADMAP
        }

        map = new google.maps.Map(document.getElementById("basic_map"), myOptions);

        var marker = new google.maps.Marker({
            position: location,
            map: map,
});
    }
    $().ready(function() {
        var geocoder = new google.maps.Geocoder();
        geocoder.geocode({ 'address': '1373 grandview ave. columbus ohio 43212'},↵
 function(results, status) {
            initialize(results[0].geometry.location);
        });
        updateLocation = navigator.geolocation.watchPosition(successGPS, errorGPS,↵
{enableHighAccuracy : true});
    });

   function successGPS(position) {
        var latlng = new google.maps.LatLng(position.coords.latitude,↵
position.coords.longitude);
        var myLocation = new google.maps.Marker({
            position: latlng,
            map: map,
```

```
            icon: bluedot,
            title:"Me"
        });
    }
    function errorGPS() {
        alert('GPS Error');
    }
</script>

<div id="basic_map" style="width:320px;height:240px;"></div>
```

When I run this example in my own location, I get the screen shown in Figure 7-5. However, if you use this code example directly, your goal will be a long way from your current position (unless you happen to be near Grandview Avenue!), so update the geocoder to a location near you to try this for yourself.

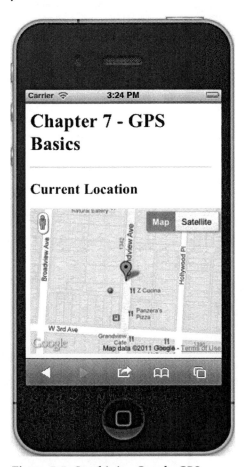

Figure 7-5. Combining Google GPS

Now you've combined everything with one simple example, including using geolocation, using geocoding, and putting two markers on a dynamic Google map. Now let's apply it to the example web app, Grandview Avenue.

Putting It All Together

So far, for our mobile Grandview Ave site we've started putting things together. We have navigation, we have a business directory, but we don't have features like near-me, parking, or the actual location of a business on the avenue. Now we are ready to do that.

Parking

Grandview Avenue has very few parking spaces for the number of businesses, and all the off-street parking might be difficult to find for new visitors to the area. So, one of the things I wanted on the site was to show people the different places to park. I visited the six largest off-street parking spots near the avenue and tagged their GPS locations with my iPhone.

For this I had two options. Option 1 was to just show a static map. It was easy and fast (since it was only an image being served from Google), and it would also keep things simple.

Option 1: Static Map

Let's create a static map by constructing a URL with six markers, all representing parking locations. Let's keep it simple by reusing objects we already know, LatLng, and just using those objects to create a string.

```
function loadParking() {

var p1 = new google.maps.LatLng(39.98376667, -83.04541944);
var p2 = new google.maps.LatLng(39.98540278, -83.04531944);
var p3 = new google.maps.LatLng(39.98600278, -83.04510000);
var p4 = new google.maps.LatLng(39.98670000, -83.04495833);
var p5 = new google.maps.LatLng(39.98721389, -83.0455);
var p6 = new google.maps.LatLng(39.98236111, -83.04553056);

var marker = '&markers=color:red|label:P|'+ p1.lat() + ',' + p1.lng();
marker += "&markers=color:red|label:P|" + p2.lat() + "," + p2.lng();
marker += "&markers=color:red|label:P|" + p3.lat() + "," + p3.lng();
marker += "&markers=color:red|label:P|" + p4.lat() + "," + p4.lng();
marker += "&markers=color:red|label:P|" + p5.lat() + "," + p5.lng();
marker += "&markers=color:red|label:P|" + p6.lat() + "," + p6.lng();

var url = http://maps.google.com/maps/api/staticmap?zoom=16&size=↵
310x415&maptype=roadmap&sensor=true
+marker;
document.getElementById('map').setAttribute('src',url);

}
```

Option 2: Dynamic Map

This option combines the dynamic map created earlier with adding multiple markers. Not only did it allow me to show where the user was relative to the nearest parking location, but users could zoom in and out relative to their current location.

This example is similar to the previous "Interacting with Google Maps via GPS" example, except now it has multiple markers set via GPS location versus the one marker that just used geocoding.

■ **Note** This might not work unless you're near Grandview Avenue. I suggest you update the following markers with a single one near your current location.

```
<script
        type="text/javascript"
        src="http://maps.google.com/maps/api/js?sensor=false"></script>
<script type="text/javascript">

    var map;
    var bluedot = new google.maps.MarkerImage('/m/images/blue_dot.png',
            new google.maps.Size(38, 38),
            new google.maps.Point(0, 0),
            new google.maps.Point(19, 19)
            );

    function loadParking() {
        var latlng = new google.maps.LatLng(39.98574444, -83.04474722);

        var myOptions = {
            zoom : 16,
            center : latlng,
            draggable: true,
            mapTypeId : google.maps.MapTypeId.ROADMAP
        };

        map = new google.maps.Map(document.getElementById("map_canvas"), myOptions);
        addMarker(new google.maps.LatLng(39.98376667, -83.04541944));
        addMarker(new google.maps.LatLng(39.98540278, -83.04531944));
        addMarker(new google.maps.LatLng(39.98600278, -83.04510000));
        addMarker(new google.maps.LatLng(39.98670000, -83.04495833));
        addMarker(new google.maps.LatLng(39.98721389, -83.04514444));
        addMarker(new google.maps.LatLng(39.98236111, -83.04553056));
        updateLocation = navigator.geolocation.watchPosition(successGPS, errorGPS,↵
{enableHighAccuracy : true});
        $("#more a").css("display","none");
    }

    function successGPS(position) {
        var latlng = new google.maps.LatLng(position.coords.latitude,↵
position.coords.longitude);
```

```
        var myLocation = new google.maps.Marker({
            position: latlng,
            map: map,
            icon: bluedot,
            title:"Me"
        });
    }

    function errorGPS() {
        alert('GPS Error');
    }

    var markerCount = 1;

    function addMarker(latlon) {
        var marker = new google.maps.Marker({
            position : latlon,
            map : map,
            icon : "http://www.google.com/mapfiles/markerP.png",
            title : "Parking "
        });
        markerCount++;
    }

    $(document).ready(function($) {
        loadParking();
    });

</script>
<div style="text-align:center;margin-bottom:50px;">
    <div id="map_canvas" style="width:320px;height:410px;margin-left:-15px;↲
margin-top:-10px;"></div>
</div>
```

You can see the blue dot in Figure 7-6 at the intersection of Grandview Avenue and 3rd Avenue.

Figure 7-6. *GrandviewAve.com parking example*

Near Me

The near-me functionality is a little more difficult; here what I wanted to do was pass in the longitude and latitude, calculate the distance of each of the businesses in the database, and then sort them by closest distance.

For performance reasons I've decided to implement the near-me functionality on the server. Basically this function takes two parameters, the latitude and longitude of your current location, and then returns a result set of businesses sorted by distance.

The first variables, $lat and $lon, represent the request variables of longitude and latitude.

The function getDistance takes as parameters two GPS coordinates and then does some mathematical calculations to return the distance in meters.

The function getFeet() converts the meters returned in getDistance to feet.

The loop sorts through the entire list of business profiles creating two arrays and then sorts the distance array by shortest number of feet.

Because the profile Array has the same index (profile_id) as the distance array, I can then print the profile information from the same key as indexed via the distance array.

Because the JavaScript will know the GPS and the server will know how to calculate, I just changed the location to the new URL once the position was known, to have a semi-interactive page. To update this near-me functionality, you can set a timeout on the page or just click Near Me again in the navigation.

```php
$lat = $_GET("lat");
$lon = $_GET("lon");
if ($lat == "") {
?>
<script type="text/javascript">
    $().ready(function() {
        updateLocation = navigator.geolocation.watchPosition(successGPS, errorGPS,↵
 {enableHighAccuracy : true});
    });
    function successGPS(position) {
        var url = "near.php?lat="+ position.coords.latitude + "&lon=" +↵
position.coords.longitude;
        location.href=url;
    }

    function errorGPS() {
        alert('GPS Error');
    }

</script>
<?
} else {
function getDistance($lat1,$lon1,$lat2,$lon2) {
    $dlat = ($lat2-$lat1)*pi() / 180;
    $dlon = ($lon2-$lon1)*pi() / 180;
    $a= sin($dlat/2)*sin($dlat/2)+cos($lat1 * pi()/180) * cos($lat2 *pi()/180) *↵
 sin($dlon/2) * sin ($dlon/2);
    $c=2 * atan2(sqrt($a),sqrt(1-$a));
    $meters = 6378140 * $c; // in meters
    return $meters;
}

function getFeet($lat1,$lon1,$lat2,$lon2) {
    $feet = getDistance($lat1,$lon1,$lat2,$lon2) * 3.28;
    return round($feet,0);
}

foreach ($profiles as $profile) {
    if (floatval($profile->gps_lat) != 0 && floatval($profile->gps_long) != 0) {
        $distance = getFeet($lat,$lon,$profile->gps_lat,$profile->gps_long);
        $distanceData[$profile->id] = $distance;
        $profileData[$profile->id] = $profile;
    }
}
asort($distanceData);

<ul data-role="listview" data-inset="true" data-theme="c" data-dividertheme="a">
<?
    foreach ($distanceData as $id => $dist) {
        $tmpProfile = $profileData[$id];
```

```php
        $name = htmlentities( $tmpProfile->name,ENT_QUOTES);
        if ($dist > 500) {
            $dist = $dist/5280;
            $dist = round($dist,1) . " mi";
        } else {
            $dist = $dist . " ft";
        }
?>
<li><a href="#profile" onclick="loadProfile(<?=$id?>)"><?=stripslashes($name)?></a>↵
<span class="ui-li-count"><?=$dist?></span></li>
<?  } ?>
</ul>
```

In Figure 7-7, you see the same list page as before, except this time all the businesses are listed in order by distance.

Figure 7-7. Grandview Ave. Near Me

Business Markers

The final thing to add on the site are business markers or some way to identify a business via Google Maps. To make this work, I needed to do the following:

1. Go to each business and tag the GPS location. This was much more accurate than geocoding.

2. I also needed a dynamic Google map with marker capability.

For this you can copy the code from the previous example using the dynamic map.

```
<script type="text/javascript" src="http://maps.googleapis.com/maps/
api/js?sensor=false">
</script>
<script type="text/javascript">
    function initialize() {
        var latlng = new google.maps.LatLng(<?=$profiles->gps_lat?>,
  <?=$profiles->gps_long?>);
        var myOptions = {
            zoom: 16,
            center: latlng,
            mapTypeId: google.maps.MapTypeId.ROADMAP
        };
        var map = new google.maps.Map(document.getElementById("basic_map"),
                myOptions);
        addMarker(latlng,map);
    }
    $().ready(function() {
        initialize();
    });

    function addMarker(latlon,map) {
      var marker = new google.maps.Marker( {
        position : latlon,
        map : map,
        icon : "http://www.google.com/mapfiles/marker.png",
        title : "Location "
      });
    }
</script>
<div id="basic_map" style="width:320px;height:240px;margin-left:-15px;"></div>
```

Figure 7-8 is a view of the business profile page towards the bottom. It shows the location of the business on the map, and you can scroll and zoom this map just like you can with a native app.

Figure 7-8. *Business profile marker example*

Chapter Summary

This concludes the chapter on GPS and Google Maps. There's a lot more to Google Maps than the few areas I've touched on in this chapter. You can find out more from the official Google API web site: http://code.google.com/apis/maps/.

Before you move on to the next chapter, you should now know how to do the following:

- Capture a longitude and latitude from your iOS device

- Create a basic Google (road) map

- Geocode your location

- Add a marker or two via GPS and geocoding to your basic Google map

In the next chapter, I break away a little from building GrandviewAve.com and focus on some of the newer features in CSS3 and JavaScript that have to do with animation and effects.

These things will add some coolness to the existing part of the mobile site we've been building and show you how to create some exciting things with your mobile app you probably didn't think were possible.

CHAPTER 8

Animation and Effects

Animations, transitions, transforms, effects: they are all really about the same thing. They get stuff to move on your screen without JavaScript.

Transitions are the transition from one CSS rule to another. So a CSS can specify position, color, size of elements; the transition or movement from one color or position to another can be done purely in CSS without the need for JavaScript to manage the values.

Transforms perform 2D and 3D rotation or movement of an element in the space of the browser's window. These are especially powerful when combined with transitions because you can get simple effects such as rotating a box or more complicated transitions in 3D.

Animations, notably key frame animations are specially designed CSS meta elements that encapsulate the entity of a transition and with specific frames and specific start and stop times. These allow for custom starting and stopping of transitions and allow for greater control with more elements.

The term *effects* is a broad term for anything fancy you might want to do with the UI some of which you could only use with images, or in the case of jQuery might involve some fadeIn() or fadeOut() type of action, causing an element to fade into or out of view.

CSS Tricks

There are a few CSS tricks we'll want to use in our iOS app because they save us from having to create images, save in number of downloads, and get us closer to a native app. To give you a taste of some of the things you can do I'll show you how to create linear and radial gradients as well as how to create a reflection of some text. You can see all of these examples in Figure 8-1.

Companion Site Reference

Example 8-1: Follow the link below to run these examples on the companion site.

```
http://www.learnhtml5book.com/chapter8/tricks.php
```

Linear Gradients

Linear gradients allow you to specify the gradual changing of one color to the next without the need for an image. In the example below I create a gradient from a color of gray (#999) to white (#fff). This is done inside a 50 × 50 pixel box with a solid black border.

```
<style>
    .grad1 {
        background: -webkit-linear-gradient(top, #999, #fff);
    }
    .demobox {
        height: 50px;
        width: 50px;
        border: 1px solid #000;
    }
</style>
<h2>Linear Gradients</h2>
<div class="demobox grad1"></div>
```

Radial Gradients

Radial gradients are similar to linear in that they save you from having to create an image, but the syntax can get tricky. Refer to the following site for a detailed explanation: http://dev.w3.org/csswg/css3-images/#ltradial-gradient .

In the example below I create a 100-pixel DIV with a radius of 50 px. This makes a blue colored sphere.

```
<style>
    .big_sphere {
        width: 100px;
        height: 100px;
        border-radius: 50px;
        background: -webkit-radial-gradient(silver, #0066cc, #000066);
    }
</style>
<h2>Radial Grandients</h2>
<div class="big_sphere"></div>
```

Reflections

Reflections can be done with images or text. In the example below I apply a linear gradient to the reflection, causing it to fade out the farther away it gets from the top of the screen.

```
<style>
    .reflect1 {
        -webkit-box-reflect: below 0px -webkit-linear-gradient(transparent,↵
 transparent 10%, silver 90%);;
    }
</style>
<h2>Reflections</h2>
<h3 class="reflect1">Reflection of Text</h3>
```

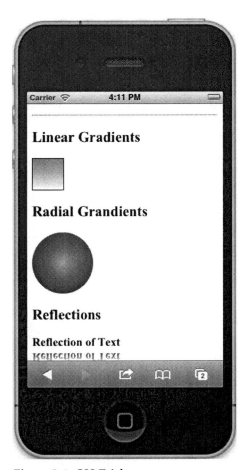

Figure 8-1. CSS Tricks

CSS Transitions

CSS transitions are the most basic kind of animation. They transition the change of state from one CSS rule to another, so if that rule is a position rule, such as `top:0px` to `top:100px`, then the transition will move the element from 0 px to 100 px without the need for JavaScript.

To use a transition you need to use the css property `-webkit-transition`. You can either use shorthand (in the example below) or you can specify each of the properties.

- `-webkit-transition-property`: This specifies the name of the property that is transitioning, such as top or left or background.

- `-webkit-transition-duration`: This is the amount of time in seconds the transition takes.

- -webkit-transition-timing-function: This specifies how the transition is timed: it can move at the same rate, it can accelerate towards the end, or slow down towards the end. Examples are: *linear, ease, ease-in, ease-out, ease-in-out,* and *cubic-bezier(n,n,n,n).*

- -webkit-transition-delay: The delay in seconds before the transition starts.

The thing you need to remember about transitions is that they can only occur on a CSS change, so something needs to force the className property of an element to change. Let's see how this works in the examples below.

Companion Site Reference

Example 8-2: Follow the link below to run these examples on the companion site.

```
http://www.learnhtml5book.com/chapter8/transitions.php
```

Simple Hover Transition

The first transition is to replace the typical :hover selector over an <a> tag. The first class demo1a, just does a standard hover. The second one demo1b, performs a transition to the new color over a one-second period.

```
<style type="text/css">
    .demo1a, .demo1b {
        color: red;
    }
    .demo1a:hover {
        color: blue;
    }
    .demo1b {
        -webkit-transition: color 1s ease-in;
    }
    .demo1b:hover {
        color: blue;
    }
</style>
<h2>Transition Demo 1</h2>
<div>
    <a href="" class="demo1a">Link Hover</a>
    <a href="" class="demo1b">Link Transition</a>
</div>
```

Simple Animation via Transition

The second transition I show moves this image from its start position at 0,0 to a new position 300,300 within the #demo2 box (Figure 8-2).

In the following transition I use the blue dot created via CSS previously versus an image. Also, rather than using JavaScript to set the new CSS className, I just use the :hover property.

■ **Note** This will not work on the iOS device because there's no concept of a mouse hover. To get this to work with iOS you need to use JavaScript to change the className.

```
<style>
#demo2 {
        width: 300px;
        height: 300px;
        border: 1px solid #000;
    }
    #demo2 img {
        position: relative;
        top: 0px;
        left: 0px;
        -webkit-transition: top 2s ease-in, left 2s ease-in;
    }
    #demo2:hover img {
        top: 280px;
        left: 280px;
    }
    .bluedot {
        width: 10px;
        height: 10px;
        border-radius: 5px;
        background: -webkit-radial-gradient(silver, #0066cc, #000066);
}
</style>

<h2>Transition Demo 2</h2>
<div id="demo2" class="change2"><img   src="images/blue_dot.png"/></div>
```

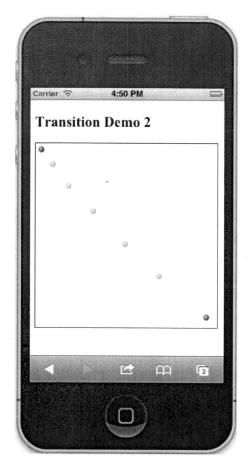

Figure 8-2. CSS Transition Example

So although this example is simple it requires no JavaScript.

■ **Note** CSS animations are faster than JavaScript animations because the CSS extensions are native to your browser and they don't have to be interpreted by your browser via JavaScript.

Flashing Image

Because we can't use the :hover property for iOS I'll actually add a single line of JavaScript to create a pulsating blue dot. For this example I just toggle the blue dot's opacity between 0 and 1 and because of the -webkit-transition property applied, this pulsates between visible and invisible every half a second.

```
<style>
    .bluedot {
        width: 10px;
```

```
        height: 10px;
        border-radius: 5px;
        background: -webkit-radial-gradient(silver, #0066cc, #000066);
        opacity:1;
        -webkit-transition-property: opacity;
        -webkit-transition-duration: .5s;
    }
</style>
<script>
    var bit = 0;
    setInterval(function() {document.querySelector(".bluedot").style.opacity=↵
bit%2;bit++},1100);
</script>
<h2>Transition Demo 3</h2>
<div id="demo3" class="change3">
    <div class="bluedot"></div>
</div>
```

CSS Transforms

The next kind of thing we do with our HTML elements is transform them from their normal position to a new one. There are two kinds of transforms we do: 2D and 3D.

CSS transforms are all about math, specifically co-ordinate systems. The 2D co-ordinate systems consist of *X*- and *Y*-co-ordinates with the *X*-axis running along the top of an element to the right and the *Y*-axis running down from the top left of the element.

For the 3D co-ordinate system we just add a third axis coming out from the page. You can think of this like the *z*-index CSS property where the higher the *z*-index, the farther out from the page an element resides.

Companion Site Reference

Example 8-3: Follow the link below to run these examples on the companion site.

```
http://www.learnhtml5book.com/chapter8/transforms.php
```

Simple 2D Rotation

In the example below I just take a normal box and rotate it 45 degrees. See Figure 8-3. To build on transitions from the previous section, I rotate it to 0 degrees when I hover over the element.

```
<style>
    .demobox {
        height: 100px;
        width: 100px;
        border: 1px solid #000;
        float: left;
        margin: 40px;
    }
    .rot45 {
        -webkit-transform: rotate(45deg);
        -webkit-transition: -webkit-transform 1s ease-in;
```

```
        }
        .rot45:hover {
            -webkit-transform: rotate(0deg);
        }
</style>
<h2>2D Transforms - Rotation</h2>
<div class="demobox"></div>
<div class="demobox rot45">45</div>
```

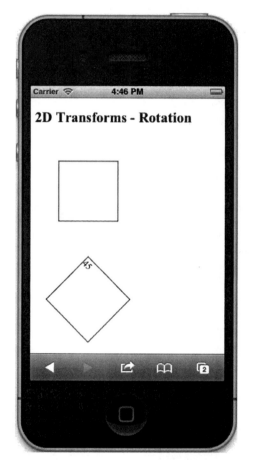

***Figure 8-3.** Simple 2D Transform w/Transition*

3D Transforms

3D transforms are just as easy as 2D but you need to be cognizant of your co-ordinate system and what you want to accomplish. If you're not careful, the effect you are trying to achieve will look strange until you get your bearings.

Next you take an image and rotate it in the 3D space, specifically 80 degrees around both the x- and the y-axes and then straighten it again on the transition out. See Figure 8-4.

```
<style>
.rotate {
        height: 200px;
        width: 300px;
        border: 1px solid #000;
        padding: 0px;
    }
    .rotate img {
        -webkit-transform: perspective(500px) rotate3d(1, 1, 0, 80deg);
        -webkit-transition: -webkit-transform 3s;
    }
    .rotate img:hover {
        -webkit-transform: rotate3d(1, 1, 0, 0deg);
    }
</style>
<h2>3D Transforms - Rotating</h2>
<div class="rotate"><img src="images/figlio.jpg"></div>
```

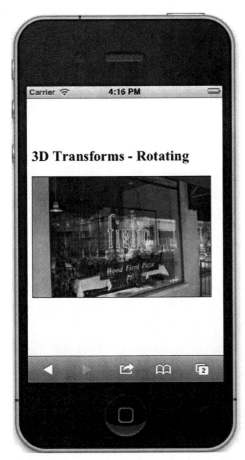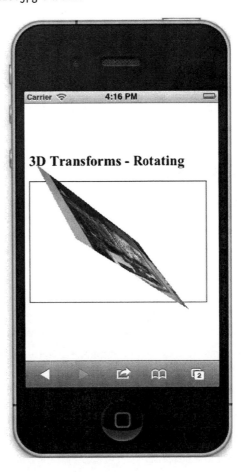

Figure 8-4. 3D Rotate Example

When you mouse over the image in Figure 8-4, the image moves in 3D. Although it might be difficult to visualize, remember you can go to the companion site to see the effect in action.

3D Flipping

The final thing we're going to do is create the "flip" effect using a transition and a transform. I've added the additional CSS properties -webkit-perspective which creates the vantage point of viewing the 3D transform.

So by rotating an element around the *Y*-axis (moving top and bottom on the page) an element will appear to be flipping from front to back around its center.

```
<style>
    .flip,.flipped {
        height: 210px;
        width: 310px;
        border: 1px solid #000;
        padding: 5px;
        background: red;
        -webkit-perspective: 800;
        -webkit-transition: -webkit-transform 1s;
    }
    .flipped {
        background: blue;
        -webkit-transform: rotateY(180deg);
    }
</style>
<h2>3D Flip</h2>
<div class="flip" onclick='this.className="flipped"'></div>
```

Key Frame Animations

Key frame animations allow for finer control of transitions into multiple steps and allow you to call transitions by name versus having to specify them by individual CSS classNames. To use these CSS declarations you use the following syntax.

```
@-webkit-keyframes THE-NAME-OF-YOUR-ANIMATION {
    0% or from {css rules}
    100% or to {css rules}
}
```

Then inside your CSS use the following property.

```
#elementid {-webkit-animation: THE-NAME-OF-YOUR-ANIMATION }
```

Now try a few examples such as changing background colors and moving elements, both of which I did earlier with a transition.

Companion Site Reference

Example 8-4: Follow the link below to run these examples on the companion site.

```
http://www.learnhtml5book.com/chapter8/animations.php
```

Changing a Background

The following example creates an animation named bgchange, and applies to the #demo1,change1 box and is set to start one second after the page loads.

```
<style type="text/css">
#demo1 {height:100px;width:100px;border:1px solid #ccc;}
@-webkit-keyframes bgchange {
  from {background: #fff;}
  to {background: #999;}
}
#demo1.change1 {
    -webkit-animation-name: bgchange;
    -webkit-animation-duration:2s;
    -webkit-animation-timing-function:ease;
    -webkit-animation-delay:1s;
    -webkit-animation-iteration-count:5;

}

</style>
<h2>Animation Demo 1</h2>
<div id="demo1" class="change1"></div>
```

Moving a Blue Dot

This example has five different keyframes, the start and final followed by three stops in between. Specifically, this animation takes the blue dot and follows the perimeter of the square and does it five times in four seconds.

```
<style type="text/css">
.demobox {height:100px;width:100px;border:1px solid #ccc;}
@-webkit-keyframes outside {
  0% {top: 0px;left:0px;}
  25% {top:0px;left:100px;}
  50% {top:100px;left:100px;}
  75% {top:100px;left:0px;}
  100% {top:0px;left:0px;}
}
.bluedot {
    width: 10px;
    height: 10px;
    border-radius: 5px;
    background: -webkit-radial-gradient(silver, #0066cc, #000066);
    position:relative;
    -webkit-animation-name: outside;
    -webkit-animation-duration:4s;
    -webkit-animation-timing-function:ease;
    -webkit-animation-delay:1s;
    -webkit-animation-iteration-count:5;
    -webkit-animation-direction:normal;
}
</style>
<h2>Animation Demo 4</h2>
<div class="demobox">
```

```
    <div class="bluedot"></div>
</div>
```

Adding a Little JavaScript

Because the hover CSS selector does not work in iOS, in order to be effective with using our animations we need to use a little JavaScript. Specifically we can use JavaScript and its events such as tap or swipe to initiate a className change, which can start an animation.

Companion Site Reference

Example 8-5. Follow the link below to run these examples on the companion site.

```
http://www.learnhtml5book.com/chapter8/addingjs.php
```

Zooming

The first thing I want to test is zooming into an element when I tap it. This can be extremely useful given the size of an iOS device when it comes to viewing high-resolution images.

　　The example below sets two classNames, scaledimg is the default class name and scaledimg2 is the image when it's zoomed.

　　For this example I've created a double resolution image to be scaled; this way the image does not pixelate when zoomed.

　　The JavaScript just uses a bit variable to toggle back and forth. In the final site I'd probably just use the jQuery toggleClass function, but the code below uses pure JavaScript.

```
<style>
    .zoom {
        width: 300px;
        height: 200px;
        border: 1px solid #000;
        overflow: hidden;
    }
    .scaledimg {
        -webkit-transform: scale(1);
        -webkit-transition: -webkit-transform 1s ease-in;
    }
    .scaledimg2 {
        -webkit-transform: scale(3);
        -webkit-transition: -webkit-transform 1s ease-in;
    }
</style>
<script>
    var zoombit = 0;
    function zoom() {
        if (zoombit == 0) {
            document.querySelector("#zoomimg").className = "scaledimg2";
            document.querySelector("#zoombutton").innerHTML = "Zoom Out";
            zoombit = 1;
```

```
        } else {
            document.querySelector("#zoomimg").className = "scaledimg";
            document.querySelector("#zoombutton").innerHTML = "Zoom In";
            zoombit = 0;
        }

    }
</script>
<h2>Zooming w/JS</h2>
<button onclick="zoom()" id="zoombutton">Zoom In</button>
<div class="zoom"><img src="images/figlio.jpg" class="scaledimg" id="zoomimg"></div>
```

Transforming (Rotating)

The second use of JavaScript is to rotate an image 360 degrees. For that you can just dynamically add the transform to the element each time you click the button Start. Also note that the added transition tells this to occur in two seconds.

You can change the number of times you want it to rotate by changing the angle size and change the speed of the rotation by changing the transition duration.

```
<style>
    .demobox {
        height: 100px;
        width: 100px;
        border: 1px solid #000;
        margin: 40px;
        -webkit-transition: -webkit-transform 2s;
    }
</style>
<script>
    var angle = 0;
    function rotateme() {
        angle = angle + 360;
        var box1 = document.querySelector("#box1");
        var asize = "rotate(" + angle + "deg)";
        box1.style.webkitTransform = asize;
    }
</script>
<h2>2D Transforms w/JS</h2>
<button onclick="rotateme()">Start</button>
<div class="demobox" id="box1"></div>
```

■ **Note** To know when your transition or animation is over add the event listeners called webkitAnimationEnd and webkitTransitionEnd. These can be added to an element or the document.

Effects with jQuery

Both jQuery and jQuery Mobile have effects and animations. All of these take the form of what's been previously described, but if you already have these frameworks on your site, it might be easier to use them rather than crafting your own transitions, transforms, and keyframe animations.

A Few jQuery Effects

These are just a few jQuery effects I've used on the present site.

- `.animate()`: A mapping of CSS properties towards which an animation will move. You combine these properties with the animation's duration, ease and what to do when it's complete.

- `.fadeIn()` : Fades the opacity of an element to one.

- `.fadeOut()`: Fades the opacity of an element to zero.

- `.hide()`: Sets the display property of an element to "none".

- `.show()`: Sets the display property of an element to "block".

- `.slideDown()`: Sets the element to slide down out of view.

- `.slideUp()`: Sets the element of the page to slide up into view.

There are also many plugins available that provide other animated functionalities you may want to use on your mobile site. Check them out at jQuery.com.

jQuery Mobile Effects

We borrowed the effects for jQuery Mobile from jQtouch with minor modifications. To invoke these transitions on a link or button just add the attribute *data-transition="value"*. Those transitions are as follows.

- `slide`: Slides to the left.

- `slideup`: Slides up into view.

- `slidedown`: Slides down out of view.

- `pop`: Pops into view.

- `fade`: Fades out of view.

- `flip`: Flips into view.

You can also change the direction of these by adding the attribute `data-direction="reverse"`.

Putting It All Together

For the Grandview.Com mobile site most of the functionality for effects is going to be provided by jQuery and jQuery Mobile. I won't write much in the way of custom animations for the site currently except for zooming of business profile images.

Right now the initial photo of a specific business is just the view of the business as it is on the street. But sometimes these images can overlap, especially if these businesses are close together.

Take, for example, Mohr Wealth Management. It's in a building shared by three other businesses, so to highlight this business I thought adding a zoom feature by tapping the photo would be a nice way to make this business stand out. For that I added the same zoom feature discussed earlier in the chapter; in fact it's the same code but with the image from the business versus the static image in the previous snippet. On the left of Figure 8-5 you see the standard picture, and on the right you see the image zoomed.

Figure 8-5. *Zoom Feature Added to Profile*

Chapter Summary

In this chapter I talked about all of the stuff generally classified as animation and effects. This is mostly CSS3 with a few JavaScript hooks allowing things to happen from specific events that occur inside the user interface of your mobile site.

Before moving on to the next chapter you should know how to do the following.

- Use some CSS tricks to make your site faster and slicker without using images.
- Create CSS transitions to change properties of your page elements.

- Use CSS transforms to rotate or move page elements in 2D or 3D space.

- Combine multiple transitions with keyframe animations.

- Hook these together with some JavaScript.

You should also be familiar with some predefined effects from jQuery and jQuery Mobile.

Of course moving predefined or fake images (via CSS tricks) can be a lot of fun. We've only scratched the surface of what you can do with HTML5. Next I'm going to talk about taking graphics to a whole new level by exploring the <canvas>.

CHAPTER 9

Canvas

Think of canvas as an image you can write on with shapes, lines, text, or other images. But not only can you write on it, but you can position, transform, manipulate, rotate, and do many other kinds of things, all with JavaScript. The <canvas> tag itself is only a container for graphics, the way a <div> or <header> is a container for text for structural or textual elements on a web page.

The <canvas> HTML element supports all the global attributes including ID and class, but adds two other attributes: width and height. These attributes take pixels as the type so a tag <canvas id="can" width="300" height="300"></canvas>, will produce a canvas of 300 × 300 pixels.

In this chapter I talk about how to do the following.

- Draw shapes and text.

- Work with images by performing real-time image processing.

- Animate those images to create the foundations for a 2D Game.

- Update the GrandviewAve.com mobile site with a 2D Game for Sales & Specials and provide for a better footer navigation.

The <canvas> element itself is very powerful, but let's start with something basic.

Canvas Basics

First in Chapter 2 I created a simple canvas element and drew a rectangle and as long as your DOCTYPE was HTML5 you were able to paste this code into any HTML page and your browser would show you a red square.

```
<canvas id="simplecanvas"></canvas>
<script type="text/javascript">
var canvas = document.querySelector('#simplecanvas');
var ctx = canvas.getContext('2d');
ctx.fillStyle='rgb(255,0,0)';
ctx.fillRect(0,0,100,100);
</script>
```

You can see from this example you need two basic objects, the canvas and the context.

Canvas Object

This object is a standard HTML element. You can reference it via `document.getElementById` or `document.querySelector(ELEMENT_ID)`. This object has two properties outside the global attributes called height and width. It has three methods:

- `toDataURL()`: Returns string data representing the image in the canvas.

- `toBlob()`: Returns a blob object representing the image in the canvas.

- `getContext()`: Returns the drawing context, currently either 2D or Experimental-WebGL (3D).

2D Context Object

This is the drawing context. It contains all the methods used to draw, rotate, and otherwise manipulate the drawing space. Some of the method categories are:

- *State:* Methods like `save()` and `restore()` change the state of the context; this is useful when transforming or clearing the context.

- *Transformations:* Methods like `scale()`, `rotate()`, `translate()`, `transform()`, and `setTransform()` all allow you to transform the objects in the context. Much as CSS transitions allow you to move objects on the screen, these allow you to move around the stuff you've drawn.

- *Rectangles:* Methods like `clearRect()`, `fillRect()`, and `strokeRect()` allow you to work with rectangles in the context.

- *Paths:* Methods like `beginPath()`, `moveTo()`, `arc()`, `fill()`, and so on are all designed to allow you to draw on your context from pixel to pixel.

- *Images:* Methods like `drawImage()`, `createImageData()`, and `getImageData()` allow you to get images from the browser or a URL, put them into your context at specific positions, and work with and manipulate them.

There are a slew of other methods and properties; for a more detailed explanation of those I'd recommend you check them out from the W3C.

`http://www.w3.org/TR/html5/the-canvas-element.html`

Now on to some examples.

Drawing Examples

The first set of examples focuses on some basic drawing. We create a few different canvas elements on the page for the different things we want to draw: rectangle, triangle, circle, and text.

Next we want to draw these when the page is done loading, and for that we specify a function in the `window.onload` event, but to start we need to add a little CSS and some HTML markup for the different example `<canvas>` elements.

Companion Site Reference

Example 9-1: Follow the link below to run these examples on the companion site.

http://www.learnhtml5book.com/chapter9/drawing.php

```
<style>
    .workarea {border: 1px solid #000;}
</style>
<h2>Rectangle</h2>
<canvas id="rectangle" class="workarea" width="150" height="150"></canvas>
<h2>Triangle</h2>
<canvas id="triangle" class="workarea" width="150" height="150"></canvas>
<h2>Circle</h2>
<canvas id="circle" class="workarea" width="150" height="150"></canvas>
<h2>Text</h2>
<canvas id="txt" class="workarea" width="300" height="50"></canvas>
<script type="text/javascript">
    window.onload = function() {
        drawRectangle();
        drawTriangle();
        drawCircle(75, 75, 50);
        drawText();
    }

</script>
```

Drawing a Rectangle

The first function draws a rectangle via the drawRectangle() function. This creates the canvas object from the document.querySelector and creates a context object which it derives from the canvas. Add this function between the <script> tags in your markup.

Once we have a context, specify the fillStyle which lets you set the color of the context, in this case red. Next you can call fillRect(xStart, yStart, xEnd, yEnd) with the parameters of the co-ordinates starting at the top left and ending at the bottom right. In the example below it creates a red square starting at 25,25, and ending at 100,100 (<canvas> co-ordinates are measured from top-left). You can see the results in Figure 9-1, along with the next example.

```
function drawRectangle() {
    var canvas = document.querySelector('#rectangle');
    var ctx = canvas.getContext('2d');
    ctx.fillStyle = 'rgb(255,0,0)';
    ctx.fillRect(25, 25, 100, 100);
}
```

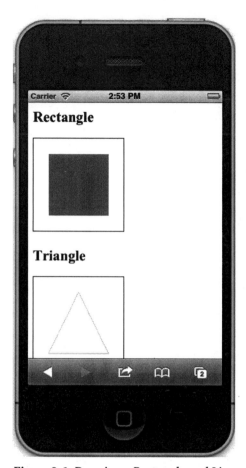

Figure 9-1. Drawing a Rectangle and Lines

Drawing with Lines

Let's draw the triangle next. Note there's no "draw shape" method available as in `drawRectangle` above; here we actually need to draw three lines.

As with the rectangle we need to grab the canvas object from the DOM and derive a context object. Next, set the color of the strokes with the `strokeStyle` method, in this case green. We start the path with `beginPath`, then move it to our first co-ordinate. This is followed by `lineTo` our second and third co-ordinates. Finally we close the path with `closePath` then `stroke` the line to create the triangle in Figure 9-1.

```
function drawTriangle() {
        var canvas = document.querySelector('#triangle');
        var ctx = canvas.getContext('2d');
        ctx.strokeStyle = 'rgb(0,255,0)';
        ctx.beginPath();
        ctx.moveTo(25, 125);
        ctx.lineTo(75, 25);
```

```
        ctx.lineTo(125, 125);
        ctx.closePath();
        ctx.stroke();
    }
```

Drawing Circles

Drawing a circle is a little bit of a combination of the two techniques we've just used. You have a method called arc which lets you specify the center in *x–y* co-ordinates, a radius and size of the arc in radians, as well as whether it should be filled or stroked. I've created a drawCircle method to shorten the amount of ceremony required to create a circle by eliminating most of it and just passing the *x–y* and radius parameters to a single function. You can also specify a lineWidth, and strokeStyle with additional parameters or constant values.

In the example below I just specify a blue circle with a line width of three pixels.

```
function drawCircle(x, y, radius) {
    var canvas = document.querySelector('#circle');
    var ctx = canvas.getContext("2d");
    ctx.beginPath();
    ctx.arc(x, y, radius, 0, Math.PI * 2, false);
    ctx.lineWidth = 3;
    ctx.strokeStyle = "rgb(0,0,255)";
    ctx.stroke();
    ctx.closePath();
}
```

Drawing Text

To draw text on the screen is very easy. It's so easy you might even consider this as opposed to creating images or using Flash for text. It will dramatically improve the speed of your mobile web app while maintaining the fonts you want to show.

In the example below I specify the font with the font method on the context. The text alignment and color are set using textAlign and fillStyle. The final method fillText() is where you put the text you want to draw followed by its position.

Because the example has text alignment of center, just place the text in the middle of the <canvas> plus a little buffer of 10 pixels. (You can remove this by using the textBaseline property.) You can see the result in Figure 9-2.

```
function drawText() {
    var canvas = document.querySelector('#txt');
    var ctx = canvas.getContext('2d');
    ctx.font = "30px Arial";
    ctx.textAlign = "center";
    ctx.fillStyle = "blue";
    ctx.fillText("This is text.", canvas.width / 2, (canvas.height / 2 ) + 10);
}
```

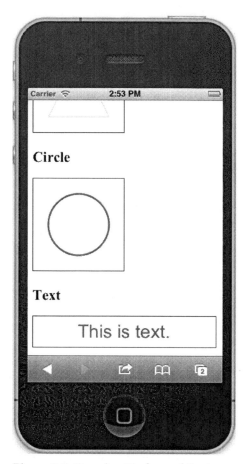

Figure 9-2. Drawing Circles and Text

Interaction Example

The next example uses a little bit from Chapter 6. Here we track a touch event and calculate a swipe event all from within the <canvas> 300 × 300 pixel element. The effect is a page that paints dots on the screen and erases them with a swipe. You can see this in Figure 9-3 or try the interaction for yourself on the companion site.

Companion Site Reference

Example 9-2: Follow the link below to run this example on the companion site.

```
http://www.learnhtml5book.com/chapter9/interact.php
```

First, we need to set up the `<canvas>`.

```
<style>
    .workarea {border: 1px solid #000; }
</style>
<h2>Touch Canvas</h2>
<p>Touch to make a dot. Swipe left to clear.</p>
<canvas id="touch_canvas" width="300" height="300" class="workarea"></canvas>
<script type="text/javascript">

    var canvas = document.querySelector("#touch_canvas");
    var ctx = canvas.getContext("2d");
    var curX,curY;

    var startX = 0;
    var startY = 0;
    var endX = 0;
    var endY = 0;

</script>
```

Next we add two events ontouchstart and ontouchend, which modify some page variables called startX, startY, endX, and endY. These variables are used to calculate whether a swipe motion was detected.

▓ **Note** I'm using 40 pixels to be sensitive to the swipe event. You might try adjusting this based on your own testing and type of interaction you prefer.

If a swipe motion is detected from within the ontouchend function, then it will clear the canvas. Otherwise the example will place a circle. You can easily adjust this to draw lines or change pen sizes and colors. The way this works is just by measuring the distance captured between touchStart and touchEnd events.

```
canvas.ontouchstart = function(evt) {
    startX = evt.pageX;
    startY = evt.pageY;
    touchXY(evt);
}

canvas.ontouchend = function(evt) {
    endX = evt.pageX;
```

```
        endY = evt.pageY;
        if ((startX - endX) < -40) {
            clearCanvas()
        }
    }
```

The helper function touchXY() allows us to update the curX and curY co-ordinates, then calls the drawCircle() function to place the circle on the canvas, Whereas drawCircle() performs the same function as the earlier example but without the radius parameter.

```
    function touchXY(e) {
        curX = e.pageX - canvas.offsetLeft;
        curY = e.pageY - canvas.offsetTop;
        drawCircle(curX, curY);
    }

function drawCircle(x, y) {
        ctx.beginPath();
        ctx.arc(x, y, 10, 0, Math.PI * 2, false);
        ctx.lineWidth = 3;
        ctx.strokeStyle = "rgb(0,0,255)";
        ctx.fillStyle = "rgb(0,0,255)";
        ctx.stroke();
        ctx.closePath();
        ctx.fill();
    }
```

To clear the canvas I just need to call clearRect from the 0,0 (top-left) to the canvas width and canvas height (bottom-right), then pop this state to the top of the canvas with the restore method.

```
function clearCanvas() {
    ctx.clearRect(0, 0, canvas.width, canvas.height);
    ctx.restore();
}
```

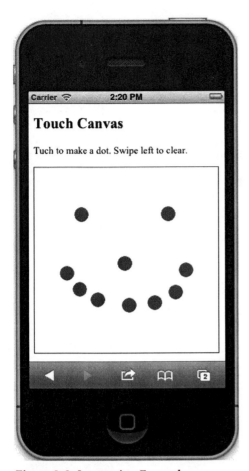

Figure 9-3. Interaction Example

Image Manipulation Example

JavaScript always had the ability to work with images as objects via the Image() object, like this:

```
var img = new Image();
img.src = "/images/some.png";
```

Using the same mechanism you can grab an image and set it to a specific location within your <canvas>.

In the following example I'll show you how you can do more with the <canvas> elements and images than just draw things. I'll show you how to do some basic image manipulation with JavaScript, so you can manipulate images without using offline or server side logic or Flash.

The first part of this example sets everything up. First create the original image called the-cangle-lab.jpg. Add a couple of buttons: *clear* which will clear the canvas and *gray* which will cause the entire source image to be converted to grayscale.

To make things a little more interactive we can create a slider which will allow us to view certain colors of gray with a range from 0 to 255.

```
<h2>Original Image</h2>
<img src="images/the-candle-lab.jpg">
<h2>Processed Image</h2>
<button onclick="clearCanvas()">Clear</button>
<button onclick="gray()">Grayscale</button>
<form>
    Threshold <input type="range" min="0" max="255" onchange=↩
"threshhold(this.value)" id="slider"/><span
        id="thresh"></span>
</form>
<br>

<canvas id="processor" width="300" height="200" class="workarea"></canvas>
```

Some Set-Up Stuff

Once the basics are set up we need to do a little housekeeping on the JavaScript and create a few global variables such as the img, canvas, and ctx.

Next, so that we populate the slider value onload we specify the innerHTML of the <span id="thresh"> tag.

```
<script type="text/javascript">
    var img = new Image();
    img.src = "images/the-candle-lab.jpg";
    var canvas = document.querySelector("#processor");
    var ctx = canvas.getContext("2d");

    window.onload = function() {
        document.querySelector("#thresh").innerHTML = document.querySelector("#slider").value;
    }

</script>
```

Next, let's create a method called gray() to create the gray effect. This method just calls the threshold function because that's where we put all the logic for making an image gray.

```
function gray() {
    threshhold(0);
}
```

In addition to clearing the canvas we also want to reset the value of the slider text and reset the slider to halfway.

```
function clearCanvas() {
    document.querySelector("#slider").value = 128;
    document.querySelector("#thresh").innerHTML = 128;
    ctx.clearRect(0, 0, canvas.width, canvas.height);
    ctx.restore();
}
```

Grayscale and Thresholding

Before getting into how to grayscale an image I want to talk a little bit about the color components of images.

First, the images we use on the web are RGB images. *RGB* stands for red-green-blue and it's the combination of these three colors that gives us all the colors we see. Images that have less green and less red are more blue, but images that have equal amounts of all three colors appear to be gray.

Just as in CSS3 you can create a color of a class by specifying green to be a rgb(0,255,0) value. You can also grab each pixel of an image and by specifying the *x*- and *y*-co-ordinates of the image you can get its component colors if you know how to look.

In addition, by knowing how to get each of these color values you can perform basic image processing such as converting an image to grayscale or creating a threshold filter. Converting the grayscale images might be trivial, however, you use the same kinds of logic if you're writing face recognition or augmented reality applications.

To create a threshold filter you just need to take a value of a color and say that you're going to do something with anything above or below this value. In the example below I first take the gray value. This is the average of the red, green, and blue components of a single pixel. Then I compare this value to a number called a threshold. Based on the numerical comparison I just convert that pixel to white or leave it alone.

The process I use below is first to grab the image data via the getImageData method, then to create a new imageData object via createImageData. Next I get these data as an array and loop through them. The array contains all the RGB information in this order.

- Data[i] = red color

- Data[i+1] = green color

- Data[i+2] = blue color

- Data[i+3] = alpha color (opacity channel)

To get the gray value I just add the RGB colors together, and then average them to get the gray value.

Finally to show the converted image, I just need to place these data into the newData array followed by the invoking putImageData method on the context.

```
function threshhold(val) {
    document.querySelector("#thresh").innerHTML = val;
    document.querySelector("#slider").value = val;
    ctx.drawImage(img, 0, 0);
    var imageData = ctx.getImageData(0, 0, canvas.width, canvas.height);
    var newImageData = ctx.createImageData(300, 200);
    var data = imageData.data;
    var newData = newImageData.data;
    for (var i = 0; i < data.length; i += 4) {
        var red = data[i]; // red
```

```
            var green = data[i + 1]; // green
            var blue = data[i + 2]; // blue
            var alpha = data[i + 3];
            var gray = (red + green + blue) / 3
            if (gray < val) {
                gray = 255; // white
            }
            newData[i] = gray;
            newData[i + 1] = gray;
            newData[i + 2] = gray;
            newData[i + 3] = alpha; // not used
        }
    ctx.putImageData(newImageData, 0, 0);
}
```

In Figure-9-4 I slid the threshold to 88 and you can see the effect this value has on the original image above it.

Figure 9-4. *Working with Images*

Animation Example

Next we try animating a few images. Specifically, I want to create a "slot-machine" effect for three images. This example just shows one image moving, but I complete the effect for three images in "Putting It All Together."

Companion Site Reference

Example 9-4: Follow the link below to run this example on the companion site.

```
http://www.learnhtml5book.com/chapter9/animation.php
```

For this example we have a button that tells the spin animation to start. The <canvas> is a 300 × 80 pixel canvas on which we place three images an equal distance apart. We can place the three images on the page initially via the window.onload event.

To set up for the spin effect we need to create a few global variables: *y* for the dynamic position of the moving image, counter to determine how many times around the canvas my image travels, and spacing which determines how many pixels the image travels per interval.

```
<style>
    .workarea {border: 1px solid #000;}
</style>
<h2>Slot Machine Example</h2>
<button onclick="callSpin()">Spin</button><br>
<canvas id="slot_canvas" width="300" height="80" class="workarea"></canvas>

<script type="text/javascript">
    var canvas = document.querySelector("#slot_canvas");
    var ctx = canvas.getContext("2d");
    var delay = 1000 / 30; // 30 FPS

    var img1 = new Image();
    img1.src = "images/grandview-cafe_thumb.jpg";

    var img2 = new Image();
    img2.src = "images/the-candle-lab_thumb.jpg";

    var img3 = new Image();
    img3.src = "images/staufs_thumb.jpg";

    window.onload = function() {
        ctx.drawImage(img1, 10, 10);
        ctx.drawImage(img2, 110, 10);
        ctx.drawImage(img3, 210, 10);
    }

    function clearCanvas() {
        ctx.clearRect(0, 0, canvas.width, canvas.height);
        ctx.restore();
```

```
    }
    var y,counter,spacing;
    function callSpin() {
        y = 10;
        counter = 0;
        spacing = 10;
        spin();
    }
</script>
```

Spinning the Images

First let's simplify some terms. The slot machine has three wheels that spin with different images. We call those w1, w2, and w3. Each wheel has the same number of images, i1, i2, and i3. Each wheel has all the images.

Spinning the wheels is nothing more than changing the position of the images i1 to i3 as time increases. To move the wheels around we just need to call the setTimeout function once. It then calls itself on every delay (which in our case is 30 frames per second or about 33 milliseconds).

Because on each call to the timeOut it increases *y* by 10, the images i1–i3 look as if they are moving around and around on a wheel.

In Figure 9-5 the first wheel is halfway between i1 and i2.

```
function spin() {
    clearCanvas();
    // slot 1
    ctx.drawImage(img1, 10, y);
    ctx.drawImage(img2, 10, y - 80);
    ctx.drawImage(img3, 10, y - 160);
    ctx.drawImage(img1, 10, y - 240);
    // slots 2&3
    ctx.drawImage(img2, 110, 10);
    ctx.drawImage(img3, 210, 10);
    // slot 1
    if (y > 240) {
        y = 0;
        counter ++;
    }else{
    y = y + spacing;
    }
    if (counter < 2) setTimeout('spin()', delay);
}
```

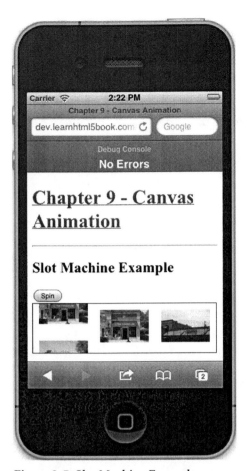

Figure 9-5. *Slot Machine Example*

Putting It All Together

So far Grandview Avenue is coming along rather nicely but it's missing something fun: it's missing a game. I had to think a little bit on what I wanted to do for a game because I've not gone and asked any of the businesses if they wanted to participate. I had ideas such as "The Avenue Hunt" which would combine with GPS in a virtual scavenger hunt. I had even thought about doing something with augmented reality, but given that it's almost winter in Ohio, I decided against spending long hours outside for testing.

So I started looking at the functionality and content that I already had on the site that needed a little spicing up and the first thing that came to mind was *Sales & Specials.* Currently I had nothing to make this page stand out and get noticed. It was just a plain old list with some information, but it did not have the coolness factor. So that was it, I needed to add the slot machine game created earlier with Sales & Specials.

The structure of the game is like this.

- Three wheels and three canvases: each slot is either a Grandview Avenue icon, or an image from one of the businesses offering a Sale & Special.

- The default icon for each of the wheels is the Grandview Ave Icon.

- There is a button that says spin at the bottom.

- Spinning causes each slot to display a random set of icons until they all stop.

- They always hit a business selected at random and "win" the Sale & Special.

One way to create these wheels is with a little Ajax to retrieve all Sales & Specials from the server and a Random() function. I've encapsulated the Sales & Specials information inside a JavaScript object called SalesSpecial.

```
<script type="text/javascript">
    var ss = [];
    function SalesSpecial(id, img) {
        this.id = id;
        this.img = img;
    }

    $().ready(function() {
        $.getJSON('/api/sales.php', function(data) {
            $.each(data, function(id, img) {
                ss.push(new SalesSpecial(id, img));
            });
        });
    });

    function getRandom() {
        return Math.floor(Math.random() * ss.length + 1);
    }

    var winner = getRandom();
    var i1 = new Image().src = ss[getRandom()];
    var i2 = new Image().src = ss[getRandom()];
    var i3 = new Image().src = ss[getRandom()];

</script>
```

Figure 9-6. *Sales & Specials Game using Canvas*

Figure 9-6 shows the finished game. To get the code for the game, go to the mobile site at http://www.grandviewwave.com/m, click on Sales and view the page source.

Chapter Summary

The goal of this chapter was to introduce you to the <canvas> element I've used to draw on and even for controlled animation via a simple slot machine game.

Before moving on to the next chapter you should know how to do the following.

- Draw lines, rectangles, circles, and images with the canvas element.

- Be able to use the canvas as a way to interact with the touch interface.

- Be able to animate with the canvas.

- Optionally you might be interested in knowing how to inspect an image for colors or be able to perform image processing.

The final piece of interactive code you need to make your mobile application complete is audio and video, and that's what I talk about next.

CHAPTER 10

Audio and Video

This is perhaps the simplest of all the chapters so far; the information here will enable you to program your HTML5 web application to render audio and video without Adobe Flash or other custom code, by using the <audio> and <video> tags and their elements.

The examples in this section are short and to the point, but the features provided by these new tags will allow you to combine a little bit of GPS to create an interactive tour for the Grandview Avenue sample app.

First I'll provide you with a short overview of these new tags.

Overview of the Audio and Video Tags

Let's take a look at the elements and attributes of the new <audio>, <video>, <source> and <embed> elements.

<audio>

The <audio> tag supports .wav, .mp3, .m4a and .acc files.

Table 10-1. Attributes of the <audio> tag.

Attribute	Value	Description
autoplay	-	Autoplays the audio when the page is ready.
controls	-	Displays the controls for the player.
loop	-	Run the audio in a loop.
preload	-	Loads the audio when the page loads.
src	url	Identifies the source of the audio to be played.

You'll see some examples incorporating the <audio> tag in iOS applications later in the chapter.

<video>

iOS supports only MPEG4 and H.264 video.

Table 10-2. Attributes of the <video> tag.

Attribute	Value	Description
audio	muted	Mutes the audio portion of the video.
autoplay	-	Autoplays the video when the page is ready.
controls	-	Displays the controls for the player.
height	pixels	Specifies the height of the player in pixels.
width	pixels	Specifies the width of the player in pixels.
loop	-	Runs the video in a loop.
poster	url	Specifies the URL of an image for the video.
preload	-	Loads the video when the page loads.
src	url	Identifies The source of the video to be played.

The following code snippet is a simple example of how to play an mp4 video file using the <video> tag. This example also uses the source child element, which we'll look at next.

```
<video width="300" controls="controls" id="myvid">
  <source src="media/grandviewave-test.m4v" type="video/mp4;" >
</video>
```

Attributes like controls don't have to take values in HTML5, but I've added them for consistency. All you need to do is enter <video controls>, and that's sufficient for the tag. Remember, this isn't XHTML.

<source>

Used in conjunction with either the <audio> or <video> tags, this child element helps to defines the source of the media.

Table 10-3. Attributes of the <source> tag.

Attribute	Value	Description
media	CSS Media Query (See Chapter 3)	Specifies what media resource is optimized for giving multiple media types for different devices.
src	url	The URL of the media.
type	Mime Type: video/mp4	The Mime type of src.

There are many different types of source media you can use with your audio and video tags.

▧ **Note** You may wonder why you need to include the Mime Type. This is so the browser can determine whether it can play the video without having to download it.

<embed>

This tag can be used to define other types of embedded content, like a `.swf` file.

Table 10-4. Attributes of the <embed> tag.

Attribute	Value	Description
height	pixels	Specifies the height of the embedded content.
src	url	The URL of the embedded content.
type	Mime Type	The Mime type of src.
width	Pixels	Specifies the width of the embedded content.

Audio and Video Examples

Before we add the audio and video elements to the Grandview Avenue sample app, here are some simple examples that will allow you to get started right away.

Using the <audio> Tag

The use of the <audio> tag is very easy.

Companion Site Reference

Example 10-1: Follow the link below to run this example on the companion site.

`http://www.learnhtml5book.com/chapter10/audio.php`

Just specify the following tag in your HTML page and that's it; you get audio played through your browser with no plugins or special software. It's as simple as that!

```
<audio src="media/audio-test-1.m4a" controls="controls" />
```

This tag includes the controls as a parameter. You can see the results in Figure 10-1.

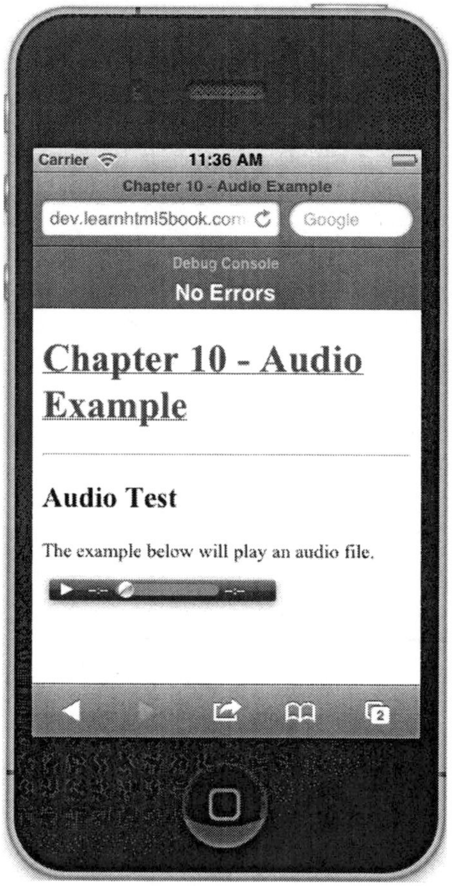

Figure 10-1. The <audio> Tag in Action

An Example Using <video> and <source>

Video is just as easy as audio, but you have more options for the video player controls and a few more attributes you can use. You can also see that in this example I used the <source> tag to specify a little bit more about the video type used, and I've used JavaScript to play it automatically on loading (onload).

Companion Site Reference

Example 10-2: Follow the link below to run this example on the companion site.

```
http://www.learnhtml5book.com/chapter10/video.php
```

```
<video width="300" controls="controls" id="myvid">
<source src="media/grandviewave-test.m4v" type="video/mp4;" >
</video>
<script type="text/javascript">
var v = document.querySelector('#myvid');
v.play();
</script>
```

Figure 10-2 shows the resulting video page. The video is set to autoplay, and the image on the right is what you will see after touching Done.

Figure 10-2. The <video> Tag in Action

Putting It All Together

To demonstrate audio and video with the Grandview Avenue app, I'd like to combine GPS with audio and video to give virtual tours. For this we'll create a number of tour locations for both audio and video elements and tag each of them to specific GPS coordinates. When the user reaches a tagged location, the appropriate tour element will play.

The basic structure of all the tours will go like this:

1. Tour Overview

2. Tour Detail (Audio and Video)

3. Tour Map (All Locations with Clickable Markers)

Creating the Tour Landing Pages

To create a tour page we'll need to use a little HTML and list functionality provided from jQuery mobile. You can see in the Landing Page 1 code that I had to modify the CSS a little bit to get it to look good (shown in bold). You might do the same or just modify the CSS of the site for the page you're on. In this section we'll also write the code that links to a map of the audio or video tour stops.

Landing Page 1

The first page just lays out and separates the audio from the video tours. Again to work around some jQuery Mobile features, I had to add <br> tags so the text would show. The links to atours.php and vtours.php are pages that represent the code in Landing Page 2.

```
<h3>Audio & Video Tours</h3>
<p style="font-size:10px;padding-bottom:10px;">Click below to take a tour of The⏎
 Avenue.</p>
<ul data-role="listview" data-theme="c" data-dividertheme="a">
    <li>
    <a href="atours.php" rel="external">
    <img src="/m/images/music-icon.png" class="ui-li-thumb" style="padding:10px;">
    <h3 class="ui-li-heading">Audio Tours</h3>
    <p>Five audio tours of Grandview <br>Avenue either sequential <br>or by nearest⏎
location.</p>
    </a></li>
    <li>
    <a href="vtours.php" rel="external">
    <img src="/m/images/video-icon.png" class="ui-li-thumb" style="padding:10px;">
    <h3 class="ui-li-heading">Video Tours</h3>
    <p class="ui-li-desc">Three video tours of Grandview <br>Avenue either sequential⏎
<br>or by nearest location.</p>
    </a></li>
</ul>
```

You can see the results on the left side in Figure 10-3.

Landing Page 2

The second landing page, once the user has chosen between audio and video tours, links to a map view of the audio or video detail.

```
<li>
<a href="amap.php#1" rel="external">
<img src="/m/images/music-icon.png" class="ui-li-thumb" style="padding:10px;">
<h3 class="ui-li-heading">South Avenue</h3>
<p class="ui-li-desc">A short description of <br>Grandview Avenue looking <br>north↵
 from First Avenue.</p>
</a></li>
```

This code displays the page shown on the right side of Figure 10-3.

Figure 10-3. *Tour Landing Pages*

When you click any link on the second landing page, you'll be taken to a map view of the page (Figure 10-4), and it will automatically play the audio file associated with the location clicked.

Tagging the Audio Tour Spots

At the end of this example, you'll see that playing the associated audio files is a fairly simple step. But before I discuss that, let's add a little GPS to identify where these tours will originate. I'm going to show you how I set up the audio tour spots, but you can see both audio and video tours in action by following the links on the companion site.

1.   1st Avenue & Grandview Avenue

2.   Staufs Coffee (On Grandview Avenue)

3.   3rd Avenue & Grandview Avenue

4.   Caribou Coffee (On Grandview Avenue)

5.   5th Avenue & Grandview

Figure 10-4. All Audio Spots on Google Map

To set-up everything to work, I'll just reuse some of the code I created in Chapter 7 (for the parking markers. All I need to do here is adjust the following addMarker statements to the locations I'll be talking about in the audio tour.

▨ **Note** If you're trying this example for yourself, remember to adjust these coordinates to some place close to you or someplace generic to the center of your map, otherwise unless you're in Grandview Heights, Ohio, the example won't work as intended.

```
addMarker(new google.maps.LatLng(39.98213, -83.0451)); // South Grandview
addMarker(new google.maps.LatLng(39.983769,-83.044948)); // Staufs Coffee
addMarker(new google.maps.LatLng(39.985027,-83.044707)); // Grandview Cafe
addMarker(new google.maps.LatLng(39.986901,-83.044939)); // Caribou Coffee
addMarker(new google.maps.LatLng(39.988613,-83.044334)); // North Grandview
```

The next important part is to link the audio files to markers on a Google map. To keep the programming simple, I'll just use the same sequence as the location markers just shown to match the file names I'll want to load and play. So as a part of the addMarker() function, I'll bind a click event to the marker so that when it's clicked or touched it will play the audio.

```
var markerCount = 1;
function addMarker(latlon) {
  var marker = new google.maps.Marker({
    position : latlon,
    map : map,
    icon : "http://www.google.com/mapfiles/markerA.png",
    title : "Audio Spot",
    clickable: true
  });

  google.maps.event.addListener(marker, 'click', function() {
    playAudio(markerCount);
  });
  markerCount++;
}

function playAudio(audioFile) {
    var audioControl = document.querySelector("#audio_control");
    audioControl.src = 'media/tour_' + audioFile + '.m4a';
    audioControl.play();
  }
```

Finally, because you will originally navigate to this page via the audio list from Figure 10-4, it will need to read the location.hash and then correctly load the audio or video file.

```
$(document).ready(function() {
  loadMap();
  playAudio(location.hash);
  });
```

Chapter Summary

The goal of this chapter was to introduce you to some new media elements for audio and video.

While using these elements was simpler than the topics covered in previous chapters, in this chapter I've started to show how you can incorporate features covered in previous chapters, like GPS, to provide some really neat functionality for your mobile web app.

Before moving on to the next chapter you should know how to

- Use the <audio> element to load audio.

- Use the <video> element to load video.

- Dynamically load and play media based on user input or other information like GPS.

While you can't take photos, video, or record voice recordings as of the current versions of iOS and Mobile Safari, there are some native services you can take advantage of, like making your iPhone beep or reading the accelerometer, and that's what I'm going to talk about next.

CHAPTER 11

Integrating with Native Services

In Chapter 7 I talked about interacting with GPS and Google Maps. But did you know in addition to GPS you can interact with the Compass, Gyroscope, and the Accelerometer on your iOS device?

What about using your web app to interact with twitter or send a text message?

This chapter tells you how to do this. Although you can't interact with your camera via Mobile Safari, I show you how to do that with a native app in Chapter 15.

Orientation

The orientation API allows you to interact with the Compass, Gyroscope, and Accelerometer on your iOS device through Mobile Safari. This makes it possible to interact with the world around you relative to the direction your device is facing and how it's moving (rotating or accelerating).

So whether you need to know what direction you're facing, or something as simple as to whether your iPhone is facing up, down, or portrait or landscape, the orientation API gives you the ability to access this information with simple JavaScript.

To access this information you need to capture the event onorientationchange. It is fired each time the device changes orientation. This is more complicated than the landscape or portrait orientation defined earlier via CSS3 media selectors. It contains a lot more information.

▒ Note For pictorial representations of the different axes please refer to the following reference.

`http://dev.w3.org/geo/api/spec-source-orientation.html`.

Properties

iOS provides five read-only properties that are passed when the onorientationchange event fires. Some are intuitive, like compass direction, but others are more complicated relative measurements based on feedback from the iPhone's gyroscope as the phone is moved.

webkitCompassHeading

This displays the direction the iOS device is pointing as you are holding it, relative to north.

- 0 degrees is North,

- 90 degrees is East,
- 180 degrees is South
- 270 degrees is West.

webkitCompassAccuracy

This provides the accuracy of the webkitCompassHeading reading. I've personally not seen it get any better than within 10 degrees of the true compass direction.

alpha (z-axis)

The alpha property is the rotation of the phone, in degrees, around its z-axis. This is the axis perpendicular to the screen (where the positive is out of the screen). The alpha property is not a compass direction; it is a relative measurement, usually based on the phone's starting position before the onorientationchange event fired.

beta (x-axis)

The beta property works in the same way as the alpha property, but it gives the rotation of the phone around its x-axis, which is the axis that runs from the left to the right of the screen.

gamma (y-axis)

Similarly, the gamma property gives the rotation of the phone around its y-axis, which is the axis running from the bottom of the screen to the top.

An Example Using Orientation

The following example updates a set of <span> tags onorientationchange. The properties are read-only and the event fires very fast.

Companion Site Reference

Example 11-1: Follow the link below to run this example on the companion site.

http://www.learnhtml5book.com/chapter11/orientation.php

```
<h2>Compass</h2>
<div>Current Heading is <span id="heading"></span></div>
<div>Compass Accuracy is <span id="accuracy"></span></div>
<div>Z-Axis(alpha) is <span id="alpha"></span></div>
<div>X-Axis(beta) is <span id="beta"></span></div>
<div>Y-Axis(gamma) is <span id="gamma"></span></div>
<script type="text/javascript">
window.ondeviceorientation = function(e) {
    var heading = e.webkitCompassHeading;
    var accuracy = e.webkitCompassAccuracy;
```

```
        var alpha = e.alpha;
        var beta = e.beta;
        var gamma = e.gamma;
        document.querySelector("#heading").innerHTML = heading;
        document.querySelector("#accuracy").innerHTML = accuracy;
        document.querySelector("#alpha").innerHTML = alpha;
        document.querySelector("#beta").innerHTML = beta;
        document.querySelector("#gamma").innerHTML = gamma;
}
</script>
```

▒ **Note** I ran this same code on my MacBook Pro and under Google Chrome I was able to receive readings from the beta and gamma elements. Try it and you can get orientation information from your MacBook Pro, but it does not work in Safari or the iOS Simulator.

Acceleration

Acceleration defines how fast your iOS device is accelerating through space. From physics, acceleration is defined as the rate of change of velocity. So even if you're going very fast this value will not change unless you're changing velocity, that is, speeding up or slowing down.

Like onorientationchange, the event ondevicemotion allows for reading the motion of your iOS device.

Properties

iOS provides four read-only properties that are passed when the ondevicemotion event fires. These are as follows.

acceleration

This object returns data in meters per second squared using the following parameters. The axes are the same ones we met earlier when looking at the alpha, beta, and gamma rotations.

- *x*: This is positive towards the right of the screen.
- *y*: This is positive towards the top of the screen.
- *z*: This is positive out of the screen.

accelerationIncludingGravity

This works the same way as the acceleration property, except with gravity factored into the result.

Interval

This is the interval in milliseconds since the last motion event.

RotationRate

This is the rate of rotation around the three axes. It uses the properties alpha, beta, and gamma like the orientation event, but measures how fast they are changing, rather than giving an overall change in degrees.

An Example Using Acceleration

This example measures the acceleration for each axis. I have also created another variable called MaxX which records the maximum acceleration in the x-direction. Most of the time while you're holding your iOS device each of these properties (acceleration.x, acceleration.y, and acceleration.z) will be below one.

Companion Site Reference

Example 11-2: Follow the link below to run this example on the companion site.

`http://www.learnhtml5book.com/chapter11/motion.php`

```
<p>Acceleration</p>
<div>X Acceleration <span id="x"></span></div>
<div>Y Acceleration <span id="y"></span></div>
<div>Z Acceleration <span id="z"></span></div>
<div>Rotation Rate <span id="rotationRate"></span></div>
<div>Max X <span id="maxX"></span></div>
<script type="text/javascript">
var maxX = 0;
window.ondevicemotion = function(e) {
    var x = e.acceleration.x;
    if (x > maxX) maxX = x;
    var y = e.acceleration.y;
    var z = e.acceleration.z;
    var rotationRate = e.rotationRate;
    document.querySelector("#x").innerHTML = x;
    document.querySelector("#y").innerHTML = y;
    document.querySelector("#z").innerHTML = z;
    document.querySelector("#rotationRate").innerHTML = rotationRate.alpha + "," +↵
 rotationRate.beta + "," + rotationRate.gamma;
    document.querySelector("#maxX").innerHTML = maxX;
}
</script>
```

Some of the ways you could use this information would be with games or augmented reality mobile web apps. Although the information above is basic, combining it with some other aspects of interactivity can be quite powerful.

Custom Links

Let's say that you want to integrate with a native app on your iOS device. What do you do? Custom APIs? Write a Native App? No. You can use *custom URLs*.

I show you several examples below on how to integrate with other apps such as mail, Facebook, or twitter and all you need to do is create a custom URL scheme with a few request parameters. If you've used `mailto:` then you're already familiar with these and don't even know it.

■ **Note** Custom URL schemes are not APIs and can change or be updated at any time. For a complete list of URL schemes go to `http://handleopenurl.com/`.

Some of the examples are built in; others you will need to have the associated applications installed on your iOS device.

Companion Site Reference

Example 11-3: Follow the link below to run these examples on the companion site.

```
http://www.learnhtml5book.com/chapter11/links.php
```

Mail

This allows you to send mail from your website via iOS Mail.

```
<p><a href="mailto:info@learnhtml5book.com">mailto:</a></p>
```

Additional URL parameters are:

```
?cc=asecond@email.com
&subject=subject_of_email
&body=body_of_email
```

For more information refer to RFC 2368; this is the URL specification guideline for `mailto` links.

SMS

The following example sends an SMS (text message) to a specific phone number. So by adding this URL link, your device will open an SMS window ready for you to write a message.

```
<p><a href="sms:1-614-555-1212">sms:</a></p>
```

MMS

The following sends a multimedia message to a specific phone number, so like SMS it opens a window, except now you have access to your multimedia SMS window.

```
<p><a href="mms:1-614-555-1212">mms:</a></p>
```

Telephone

The following allows you to call a phone number.

```
<p><a href="tel:1-614-555-1212">tel:</a></p>
```

▓ **Note** iOS will do this automatically if it detects a sequence of numbers resembling a phone number. To turn this off you must use the following meta tag, **<meta name = "format-detection" content = "telephone=no">**.

Printing

The following line prints a page.

```
<p><a href="javascript:window.print()">print</a></p>
```

Music

The following opens your music library.

```
<p><a href="music://">Music</a></p>
```

Maps

The following opens Google Maps.

```
<p><a href="http://maps.google.com?q=43212">maps.google.com</a></p>
```

YouTube

The following opens a video on YouTube.

```
<p><a href="http://www.youtube.com/v/video">www.youtube.com</a></p>
```

iTunes

The following opens an app in iTunes.

```
<p><a href="itms://itunes.apple.com/us/app/grandview-ave/id393904245?mt=↵
8">iTunes</a></p>
```

Facebook

The following opens up your Friends in Facebook.

```
<p><a href="fb://friends">Facebook</a></p>
```

Twitter

The following opens up a specific user in twitter.

```
<p><a href="twitter://user?screen_name=scottpreston">Twitter</a></p>
```

Putting It All Together

I would like to have a little augmented reality (AR) in the Grandview Avenue mobile site, but I don't quite have enough data to pull off a full-blown AR app and I can't really interact with the Camera the way I'd like to. However, I do have one idea: a hidden feature called an Easter Egg.

The Easter Egg

1. You are on the home screen and standing in the parking lot of the Grandview Avenue Carry Out on Third and Grandview Ave.

2. You point your phone towards Grandview Café.

3. The page will change to a panoramic photo of Grandview Avenue from the corner of Third and Grandview Avenue.

The Technical Parts

- I need a few images to create my panoramic shot. Assuming I get a 30-degree view per image, I need nine images for a complete 360-degree view. I then stitch these together for a single JPG and make sure that when I connect the first and ninth image they line up perfectly.

- I need to use either CSS or Canvas to move the image based on the direction in which the phone and camera are pointing (the "heading").

- I need to use the onorientationchange event to move my image and keep it in sync with the heading of the camera.

- To escape you can just use the "back" button.

The AR Code

In the following example I use the heading and tilt around the x-axis (beta) to move my image.

The first part of the code sets up the planner `<div>` with a background called `pan1.jpg`. This is the image I created: a single panorama background image of 3,072 × 673 pixels. I set the initial background positions to be 0% and 0%.

As part of the dynamic update of the CSS position I just normalize the headings and the tilt and then reset the positions using percentages.

```
<style>
    body {margin:0;}
    #panner {
        height: 480px;
        width: 320px;
        background-size: 3072px 673px;
        background-repeat: repeat-x;
        background-position: 0% 0%;
        background-image: url('images/pan1.jpg');
    }
</style>
<div id="panner"></div>
```

Next I need to create a few variables, one a global variable called heading that I can check on each GPS location to find the direction in which the phone is pointing. The second, showEgg, is a Boolean that decides whether to show the Easter Egg.

This is followed by the panImg function which changes the background position of the image as the orientation changes.

The rest of the JavaScript checks for orientation and GPS location to fire the egg when the user is in the correct position and pointing his phone towards Grandview Café.

```
<script type="text/javascript">
var heading;
var showEgg = false;

function panImg(x,y) {
    var panElt = document.querySelector("#panner");
    panElt.style.backgroundPosition = x + "% " + y + "%";
}

window.ondeviceorientation = function(e) {
    heading = Math.round(e.webkitCompassHeading);
    if (showEgg) {
        var headingAsPercent = (heading/360) * 100;
        var beta = Math.round(e.beta);
        var betaAsPercent = (Math.abs(90-beta) / 30) * 100;
        panImg(headingAsPercent,betaAsPercent);
    }
}

function successGPS(position) {
    var lat = position.coords.latitude;
    var lon = position.coords.longitude;
    var isNearEgg = testDistance(39.98600278, -83.04510000, lat, lon);
    if (isNearEgg & (heading > 90 && heading < 180 ) {
        showEgg = true;
    }
}

function testDistance(lat1, lon1, lat2, lon2) {
    var lat = lat1 * 10 ^ 6 - lat2 * 10 ^ 6; // increased size to avoid rounding
    var lon = lon1 * 10 ^ 6 - lon2 * 10 ^ 6; // increased size to avoid rounding
    if ((lat ^ 2 + lon ^ 2) ^ .5 < 100) { // close to area
        return true;
    }
    return false;
}

function errorGPS() {
    alert('GPS Error');
}

function watchGPS() {
    navigator.geolocation.getCurrentPosition(successGPS, errorGPS,↩
{enableHighAccuracy : true});
```

```
        setTimeout("watchGPS()",30000);
}

</script>
```

Figure 11-1. Grandview Avenue Easter Egg

To test this without being near Grandview and Third you can go to the URL, http://www.grandviewave.com/m/egg.php. You can view source and get all the code or just cut and paste what's above, replacing your co-ordinates with those above. Or if you just want to view the Easter Egg, you could hard-code the showEgg variable to always return true.

Chapter Summary

In this chapter I was able to show you how to use a few more native features of your iOS device to capture and use the orientation and acceleration via JavaScript. I also showed you how to integrate with external apps via URL Schemes.

Before moving on to the next chapter you should know how to do the following.

- Use the ondeviceorientation event to detect the heading of your iOS device.

- Use the ondevicemotion event to detect your iOS device moving through space.

- Use a URL scheme to integrate with some native feature or native application on your device.

Up until now we've done everything online and retrieved everything we need from the network. But sometimes the network is not going to be available or not going to be as fast as we would like it, so offloading some of the storage to the client might be a good idea, and that's what I talk about next.

CHAPTER 12

Offline Apps and Storage

There's a variety of ways to speed up your application by cacheing certain amounts of data on the client. Before HTML5 you could only store cookies or rely on the browser's cacheing mechanism. Now you can implement a variety of ways, by storing long-term data via the `localStorage` object, session data via the `sessionStorage` object, or even an entire application via `applicationCache`. Depending on the kind of application you are writing you may use none or all of these features.

The first mechanism I discuss is how to take your entire application offline, or in the case of no network, a way to make your web app work entirely in offline mode. Some HTML5 books talk about WebSQL, or the ability to access SQLite via JavaScript. I do not talk about Web SQL because this API is no longer active. If you want to find out more about this API you can reference it at: `http://www.w3.org/TR/webdatabase/`. Personally I found this a very complicated means for accessing data on the client when compared to local and session storage options discussed later in the chapter.

The Cache Manifest

This is the name of the file you create when you want your application to be permanently cached or you want it to run in offline mode. So just as with an HTML, CSS, or JS file, you need to create a .manifest file that you can place on your local system. Now this file can either be static or you can "fake" it by just specifying a MIME type. This way your browser knows how to treat it. Your web server may or may not have the MIME type installed. If it doesn't, add this to your apache configuration.

```
AddType text/cache-manifest .appcache
```

Remember, a manifest file is just plaintext as far as a text editor is concerned, nothing fancy. You can cut and paste the contents from the companion site right into your own sample application with minor modifications to file names and paths. Creating a manifest is really easy, just add the manifest attribute to your `<html>` tag such as: `<html manifest="chapter12.manifest">`.

This file has three sections: **CACHE**, **FALLBACK**, and **NETWORK**.

- The **CACHE** section is default and all the files under this section will be cached.

- The **FALLBACK** section is a list of optional pages in case a resource is not available.

- The **NETWORK** section is a whitelist of all files that require a network connection.

■ **Note** The page where the manifest is specified is always cached regardless of the .manifest file.

A Manifest Example

Below I show you a number of example files that allow for local application cacheing. After you've specified your manifest in your <html> tag you can use the information below to implement it yourself.

The next file is the manifest file, which is specified in the HTML tag of the document. This file tells the browser which files to cache and is divided into sections.

chapter12.manifest

```
CACHE MANIFEST
# v3 - 2011-11-25
# This is a comment.

CACHE:
/chapter12/index.php
/chapter12/css/ch12.css
/chapter12/js/ch12.js
/chapter12/images/akada-salon_thumb.jpg
/chapter12/images/grandview-cafe_thumb.jpg
/chapter12/images/jenis-ice-cream_thumb.jpg
/chapter12/images/the-candle-lab_thumb.jpg
/chapter12/images/the-grandview-theater_thumb.jpg
```

The problem with this is that in order to force your browser to get a new file, even if it's a dynamic page, you need to update your manifest file for each and every request. To do that I modified the manifest to be a dynamically created PHP file. For this make sure to change the name of your dynamic file, in my case chapter12.manifest.php. You can see that I've done this on the companion site example.

I'm still sending out the MIME type of text/cache-manifest, and I'm immediately expiring the file by setting the expires header to a date in the past; also I'm dynamically creating a comment in the file to keep it different each and every time.

Now if the user is offline, the next time that a browser tries to access this manifest file the dynamic update won't retrieve an update, and the content/application will come exclusively from the cache.

■ **Note** This is the same as the previous file, but I'm using PHP to set/update the cache of the manifest file.

---

chapter12.manifest.php

```
<?
header("Cache-Control: max-age=0, no-cache, no-store, must-revalidate");
header("Pragma: no-cache");
header("Expires: Sat, 01 Jan 2011 00:00:00 GMT");
header('Content-type: text/cache-manifest');
?>
CACHE MANIFEST
#comment - date is <?=date('c')?>
CACHE:
/chapter12/index.php
/chapter12/css/ch12.css
/chapter12/js/ch12.js
/chapter12/images/akada-salon_thumb.jpg
/chapter12/images/grandview-cafe_thumb.jpg
/chapter12/images/jenis-ice-cream_thumb.jpg
```

```
/chapter12/images/the-candle-lab_thumb.jpg
/chapter12/images/the-grandview-theater_thumb.jpg
```

Application Cache

This is the actual DOM object you access programmatically via JavaScript. A brief overview of the API of this object follows.

Update Statuses (read-only attribute *status*)

- UNCACHED = 0
- IDLE = 1
- CHECKING = 2
- DOWNLOADING = 3
- UPDATEREADY = 4
- OBSOLETE = 5

Updates

- update():Tells browser to invoke application download process.
- abort(): Tells browser to stop downloading and cancel updating cache.
- swapCache(): Tells browser to check the manifest and swap accordingly.

Events

- onchecking: Browser is checking for an update.
- onerror: Manifest error, or 404 of manifest file.
- onnoupdate:Manifest has not changed.
- ondownloading: Found an update and is downloading.
- onprogress: Downloading files in manifest.
- onupdateready: Files in manifest have been redownloaded.
- oncached: All files downloaded and cached.
- onobsolete: Manifest no longer exists so cache is being deleted.

An example of how to access and use this API follows. Here I am just setting up an event listener to the event updateready, and then I prompt the user to see if he would like to load the new cache into the page.

Companion Site Reference

Example 12-1: Follow the link below to run this example on the companion site.

```
http://www.learnhtml5book.com/chapter12/manifest.php
```

```
<script type="text/javascript">
    function reload() {
        window.location.reload();
    }
    // example of how to use applicationCache
    var cache = window.applicationCache;
    cache.addEventListener('updateready', function(e) {
        if (cache.status == window.cache.UPDATEREADY) {
            cache.swapCache();
            if (confirm('load new cache?')) {
                reload();
            }
        }
    });
</script>
```

In Figure 12-1 I show an example file of Chapter 12 along with all of the events that are fired from the JavaScript Console.

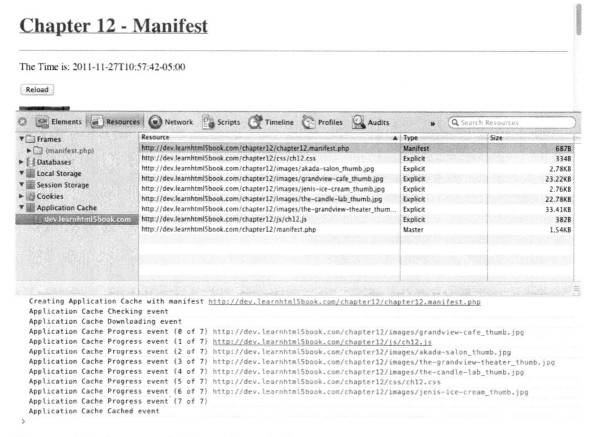

Figure 12-1. Application Cache View with Google Chrome

You use this if your application relies heavily on images or might be used frequently in a nonnetworked mode.

Cookies

In addition to the application cache there are other ways to store information on the client. The oldest way to do this is with cookies. Cookies allow you to store up to 2,048 bytes of data for a specific domain. You can set these programmatically via your server side code or via JavaScript.

Companion Site Reference

Example 12-2: Follow the link below to run this example on the companion site.

`http://www.learnhtml5book.com/chapter12/cookies.php`

In the example below I set two cookies. Cookie A is going to be a session cookie. Cookie B is going to be a semi-permanent cookie that expires in 30 days.

```
<button onclick="setCookie('test1','A')">Set Cookie A</button>
<button onclick="setCookie('test2','B',30)">Set Cookie B</button>
<script type="text/javascript">
    function setCookie(name, value, expire_days) {
        var expire = new Date();
        expire.setDate(expire.getDate() + expire_days);
        var value = escape(value) + ((expire_days == null) ? "" : "; expires=" +↵
expire.toUTCString());
        document.cookie = name + "=" + value;
    }
</script>
```

Figure 12-2 shows you these two cookies: one with an expiration date and another which is a session cookie.

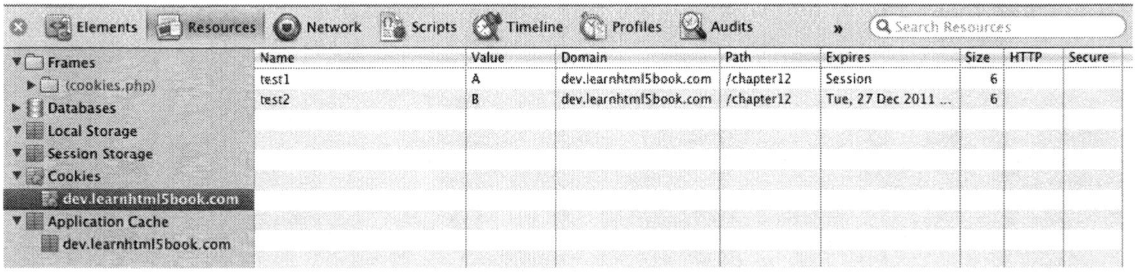

	Name	Value	Domain	Path	Expires	Size	HTTP	Secure
▼ ☐ Frames	test1	A	dev.learnhtml5book.com	/chapter12	Session	6		
▶ ☐ (cookies.php)	test2	B	dev.learnhtml5book.com	/chapter12	Tue, 27 Dec 2011 ...	6		
▶ ▊ Databases								
▼ ▊ Local Storage								
▼ ▊ Session Storage								
▼ ☐ Cookies								
▊ dev.learnhtml5book.com								
▼ ▊ Application Cache								
▊ dev.learnhtml5book.com								

Figure 12-2. Cookies with Google Chrome

Local Storage

A better way of storing content on the client is with the localStorage object. Here instead of 2 k of information we have up to 5 MB of data we're allowed to store locally. Also we're not limited to just storing strings; we can store objects just as easily.

- To put objects into local storage just use localStorage.setItem(key,value).

- To get objects from localStorage just use getItem(key).

- To remove objects from localStorage just use removeItem(key).

In the example below I'm storing one string and one object, and on loading of that object, I'm alerting it to the screen.

Companion Site Reference

Example 12-3: Follow the link below to run this example on the companion site.

http://www.learnhtml5book.com/chapter12/local.php

```
<button onclick="localStorage.setItem('test1','this is a test');">Set Local A</button>
<button onclick="localStorage.setItem('test2',new TestObject());">Set Local B</button>
<script type="text/javascript">
    function TestObject() {
        this.id = 1;
        this.name = "test object";
        this.description = "this is a test object i am going to put into local storage";
    }

    window.onload = function() {
        alert(localStorage.getItem('test1'));
    }
</script>
```

In Figure 12-3, I show the resource view of the localStorage object, where the key test2 is an object and the key test1 is just a string.

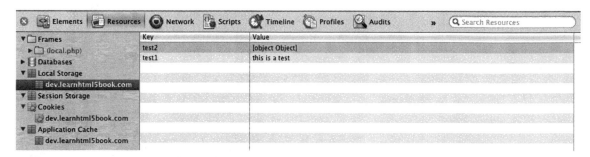

Figure 12-3. Local Storage with Google Chrome

Session Storage

To store only items per session, just use `sessionStorage` instead of `localStorage`. The methods are the same: `setItem`, `getItem`, `removeItem`, and the only difference is we store these per user session instead of over multiple sessions.

In the example below I do the same thing, except this time if you close your browser and come back you won't be greeted by the alert message until you've set it from within the current session.

Companion Site Reference

Example 12-4: Follow the link below to run this example on the companion site.

`http://www.learnhtml5book.com/chapter12/session.php`

```
<button onclick="sessionStorage.setItem('test1','this is a test');">Set Session↵
 A</button>
<button onclick="sessionStorage.setItem('test2',new TestObject());">Set Session↵
 B</button>
<script type="text/javascript">
    function TestObject() {
        this.id = 1;
        this.name = "test object";
        this.description = "this is a test object i am going to put into local storage";
    }

    window.onload = function() {
        alert(sessionStorage.getItem('test1'));
    }
</script>
```

Likewise in Figure 12-4 I view session storage from the resources menu from within Google Chrome, where key `test2` is an object and `test1` is just a string.

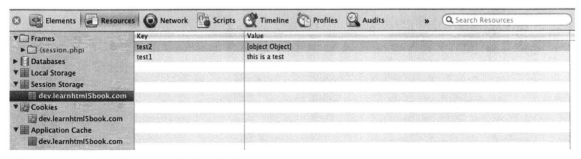

Figure 12-4. *Session Storage with Google Chrome*

Putting It All Together

Currently the Grandview Avenue app has relied exclusively on the network for everything and although the Avenue is in a 3G/4G area it might be a good idea to cache some stuff locally for better performance.

The only really data-intensive part of the application comes at the beginning where I'm getting all the profiles and associated data. So perhaps if I cache all the information for each of the business profiles it would speed up rendering of each of the profile pages. This file is perhaps about 120 k but it makes retrieval of the profile information near instantaneous versus a few seconds per profile.

To solve this problem I like to use `sessionStorage` over `localStorage` because the data update often enough (daily) but not so often that I constantly need to check for updates and maintain synchronization.

Because I'm using jQuery, I just use the `$().ready()` function to be consistent in usage versus `window.onload` from some of the previous examples. Then it's just a matter of checking for null to see if the profile data have been loaded into memory.

```
<script type="text/javascript">
    var profileData;
    if (sessionStorage.getItem('profileData') != null) {
        profileData = sessionStorage.getItem('profileData');
    }

    $().ready(function() {
        if (sessionStorage.getItem('profileData') == null) {
            $.getJSON('api/allprofiles.php', function(data) {
                sessionStorage.setItem('profileData'),data);
            });
        }
    });
</script>
```

■ **Note** I'm not able to use JSON in the Example Application because of jQuery Mobile. The framework is problematic in its current version as it does not like to reapply styles to list from dynamically created elements. Please note this is a work in progress and should a solution present itself after the publication of this book, I'll make sure to note it on the companion website.

Chapter Summary

In this chapter I showed you how to leverage some client-side storage to make your application perform faster or even work while it's offline. Before moving on to the next chapter you should know how to:

- Create and use the manifest for taking applications offline.
- Use the `applicationCache` object for managing your cached application.
- Use `localStorage` for storing simple data or objects.
- Use `sessionStorage` for storing simple data or objects.

Until now we've dived right into building our application and all of it was against my nature because I've not written a single test for any of this code. However, I plan on fixing that in the next chapter by talking about testing your mobile app. This covers topics such as unit testing with Jasmine and simulating a slow network through the iOS simulator.

CHAPTER 13

Mobile Testing

A few years back at a conference I heard this analogy between modern software engineers and civil engineers. The story went something like this: suppose you were building a bridge that had never been built before and you were using a new architecture on which the previous equations you used to solve bridge problems did not apply. How would you know if the bridge could support the proposed weight?

One group of people began solving the problem by going about trying to refactor their equations to solve the problem.

A second group of people solving the problem went about it slightly differently. They built a sample of the bridge, and they loaded it until it broke. They repeated this over and over until they found the capacity of the bridge.

In software we like to use the second way too; we like to test. These tests range from unit-testing custom APIs to testing the performance of your web server and API. This testing provides valuable insight into your application and you should not launch or even start building your application without setting up your test.

Before writing this book I debated whether to make this the first chapter in the book because "test-driving code" has been a practice I use to make my code better and myself a better programmer. In this chapter I talk about the following kinds of testing.

- Unit testing with Jasmine

- Performance testing with benchmarking, load testing, and simulating a mobile network

- Automated testing with Watir

- A/B testing

But first I'd like to talk about a few terms: TDD, or test-driven development, and BDD, behavior-driven development.

Test-Driving Code

Long before the practice of TDD the practice of creating software went something like this.

- Write some code.

- Write some more code.

- If you have time write a test for your code.

- If it breaks fix it fast, and push it live.

Developers didn't write test because code usually worked or they used an excuse such as "they had if statements" in the code to check for errors. Other reasons for not testing might be "testing would slow me down" because it would often take less time to fix a bug than to write a comprehensive test for a piece of code.

But what happens if you can't have downtime? What happens if you need to refactor a lot of your code and can't afford to find out where it breaks because you can't have downtime?

For these cases you write a test. The practice of writing test-first was introduced as test-driven development.

TDD or Test-Driven Development

Test-driven development or TDD is the practice of:

1. Write a test.

2. Watch it fail.

3. Fix your code so test will pass.

4. Refactor your code.

5. Repeat Step 1.

By writing your test first you truly understand the acceptance criteria or requirements of your component or application. I use TDD in the example below.

Step 1

The first thing I write is a function assertString(). This takes two parameters: an expected value and an actual value; it compares the two and returns a true if they are the equal.

Step 2

Next, I write a testHello function and drop it into the onload event.
The first time I run this it fails.

Step 3

Next, I write the hello function with nothing in it, and guess what, it fails again.
Finally, I write the hello function with a string parameter so that it returns hello followed by the hello string plus the name variable passed in. Now when I run the test or refresh the page the test passes. This is TDD.

Companion Site Reference

Example 13-1: Follow the link below to run this example on the companion site.

http://www.learnhtml5book.com/chapter13/tdd.php

```
<script type="text/javascript">
// step 1
    function assertString(expected, actual) {
        return (expected == actual);
    }

// step 2
    window.onload = function testHello() {
        if (assertString("hello scott", hello("scott"))) {
            alert("hello works");
        } else {
            alert("hello fails");
        }
    }
// step 3
    function hello(name) {
        return "hello " + name;
    }
</script>
```

Sometimes these tests are very developer-centric and their meaning can get lost in translation (translation to your business team). To compensate for this, a different type of semantics would be needed to cross boundaries of developers, quality assurance, and business. Along came behavior-driven development or BDD.

BDD or Behavior-Driven Development

Behavior-driven development or BDD is very close to TDD except the language and semantics normally used in TDD are replaced with business- and user-centric terms that make sense to everyone on your team, not just developers. An example of the previous "hello" example would look like this as a BDD test case:

```
Given a user visits a page named "scott",
Then the user should be greeted with an alert called "hello scott".
```

In order to provide consistency a language was created for this called **Gherkin**. Gherkin is used in **Cucumber** for Ruby, **Lettuce** for Python, **Speclow** for .NET, and **behat** for PHP. All of these are BDD unit-testing frameworks that allow for automated integration and unit testing.

Gherkin consists of the following.

- **Features** that describe a single characteristic of a piece of software.

- **Scenarios** that are comprised of steps to test a feature.

- **Steps** consisting of Givens, Whens, and Thens.

- **Givens** are designed to put the system into a known state and are where your assumptions are created.

- **Whens** describe key actions such as when I click a button or enter certain text.

- **Thens** describe the outcomes or what to expect.

For more information on Gherkin, view its website at

```
https://github.com/cucumber/cucumber/wiki/Gherkin
```

In the previous example I wrote my own assertion and test but it provided no means to actually test anything. So how do you get from a few English sentences in Gherkin to doing behavior-driven development? Fortunately there is a JavaScript unit testing framework that provides both kinds of assertions I want to use for my JavaScript unit test as well as BDD Gherkin interpreters that allow for real unit tests and that's called Jasmine.

Unit Testing with Jasmine

Jasmine is a BDD framework for testing JavaScript. You can download and read more about Jasmine at: `http://pivotal.github.com/jasmine/`. To install just unzip the files and follow the instructions below, moving the files into the relevant directory for your project.

Companion Site Reference

Example 13-2: Follow the link below to run this example on the companion site.

`http://www.learnhtml5book.com/chapter13/jasmine.php.`

To get started I show you a simple example. First the basics: you need to include the `jasmine.css`, `jasmine.js`, and `jasmine-html.js` files at the top of your test harness. A test harness is just a web page where you can include the files you're going to test.

```
<link rel="stylesheet" type="text/css" href="js/jasmine.css">
<script type="text/javascript" src="js/jasmine.js"></script>
<script type="text/javascript" src="js/jasmine-html.js"></script>
```

Next I add my function (it's the same `hello()` function as before).

```
<script type="text/javascript">
    // the function part (your code)
    function hello(name) {
        return "hello " + name;
    }
</script>
```

Now I write my spec, short for specification. This has three parts: `describe`, `it`, and `expect`.

- The `describe` part is a way to group different specs together.

- The `it` part is the specification.

- The `expect` is short for expectations. This is for expressing what you expect from the code.

In the code below we're expecting the call to `hello('scott')` to return a string `"hello scott"`.

```
<script type="text/javascript">
    // the spec part
    describe('hello()', function() {
        it('says hello', function() {
            expect(hello('scott')).toEqual("hello scott");
        });
```

```
    });
</script>
```

As before in TDD, our first test should fail, so to implement it in Jasmine, we write some code to execute our specification defined above. After running it we get the output shown in Figure 13-1.

```
<script type="text/javascript">
    jasmine.getEnv().addReporter(new jasmine.TrivialReporter());
    jasmine.getEnv().execute();
</script>
```

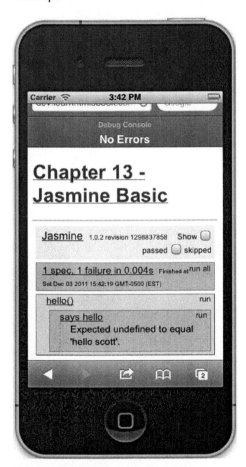

Figure 13-1. Showing failing test

Next I add the hello function and get a passing test, shown in Figure 13-2.

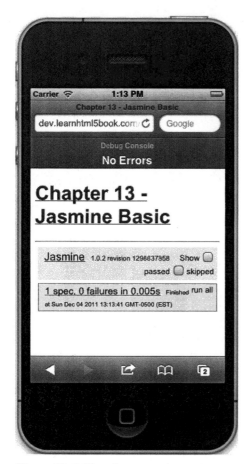

Figure 13-2. Showing a passing test

To use Jasmine with your mobile site, build a suite of test harnesses for all of your custom JavaScript. We look at using Jasmine with Grandview Ave later, in "Putting It All Together."

Performance Testing

Performance testing or page performance testing is different from load testing in that it measures the performance of the page load and JavaScript running on the client browser, not the speed at which your web server can serve text, images, or other media.

Performance testing becomes important because your iOS device will run JavaScript a little to a lot slower than the MacBook with which you're developing your website. Before I talk about the test I actually show you some results; they might surprise you.

First I create a few different kinds of test:

- *Simple Test:* Counting a million times in a loop
- *Native JavaScript:* DOM Traversal
- *JQuery:* DOM Traversal

Second, in Table 13-1 we compare them on the iPad v1, iPhone4, Chrome 15, and Safari 5.1.2. This will give you relative feel for how they compare against one another.

Table 13-1. Performance Comparison

Test	iPad v1 (ms)	iPhone4 (ms)	Chrome v15 (ms)	Safari 5.1.2 (ms)
Simple	13	19	2	2
Native JS	432	541	87	183
jQuery 1.6.4	567	705	83	213

The Benchmark Object

Before taking benchmarks, I create a simple JavaScript object to calculate the time between two events, start and stop. The benchmarking object will need to measure time in milliseconds. The following example creates a benchmark object with properties startTime and endTime and has the methods, start, stop, and get.

Companion Site Reference

Example 13-3: Follow the link below to run this example on the companion site.

http://www.learnhtml5book.com/chapter13/benchmark.php

```
<script type="text/javascript">
    function Benchmark() {
        this.startTime = "";
        this.endTime = "";
        this.start = function() {
            this.startTime = new Date().getTime();
        };
        this.stop = function() {
            this.endTime = new Date().getTime();
        };
        this.get = function() {
            return this.endTime - this.startTime;
        };
    }
</script>
```

Now I'll talk about three separate performance tests: one is for a simple loop and the other two compare native selectors and the jQuery selector as I iterate through and update the DOM.

Simple Loop

This is a simple loop that counts 1 million times and does nothing else.

```
<script type="text/javascript">
 function test1() {
        var foo = new Benchmark();
        foo.start();
        for (var i = 0; i < 1000000; i++) {
        // do nothing
        }
        foo.stop();
        alert("1,000,000 loops take " + foo.get() + "ms.");
        location.reload();
    }
</script>
```

DOM Traverse and Modify

The DOM traversal iterates through 10,000 <div> elements. To set up the DOM Traversal test I create the following HTML and 10,000 <div> elements using PHP.

```
<script src="/js/jquery-1.6.4.min.js"></script>
<button onclick="test1()">Simple Test</button>
<button onclick="test2()">Native Selector</button>
<button onclick="test3()">jQuery Selector</button>
<?php for ($i=0;$i<10000;$i++){?>
<div id="<?=$i?>" class="foo"><?=$i?></div>
<?}?>
```

First I use the native querySelector to grab all classes then modify all the innerHTML of these elements. I then alert the time and reload the page so as to avoid any browser caching.

```
<script type="text/javascript">
function test2() {
        var foo = new Benchmark();
        foo.start();
        var divs = document.querySelectorAll(".foo");
        for (var i = 0; i < divs.length; i++) {
            var elt = divs[i].innerHTML = "foo"+i;
        }
        foo.stop();
        alert("native selector time is " + foo.get() + "ms");
        location.reload();
    }
</script>
```

DOM Traverse and Modify w/jQuery

This does the same thing as the previous example and makes use of the .each() function from within jQuery.

```
<script type="text/javascript">
function test3() {
        var foo = new Benchmark();
```

```
        foo.start();
        $('.foo').each(function(index, elt) {
            elt.innerHTML = "foo"+index;
        });

        foo.stop();
        alert("jquery selector time is " + foo.get() + "ms");
        location.reload();
    }
</script>
```

A Short Note on Network Throttling

One thing that it will be difficult to test your web app with will be to simulate 3G or slower speeds.

To get around this your Mac has the ipfw command, which is short for IP Firewall. To get your Mac to slow down the speed at which it accesses a network resource, just open a terminal then enter the following commands.

```
sudo ipfw pipe 1 config bw 4KBytes/s
sudo ipfw add 1 pipe 1 src-port 80
```

To remove this restriction enter the following command.

```
sudo ipfw delete 1
```

To test this out I created the following large file (~100 k). This can be any random file name; I used large.php.

```
<?php
for ($i=0;$i<100000;$i++) {
echo 'a';
}
?>
```

Using this file, try executing the following Ajax Request using jQuery. This test loads a large file via AJAX (previous file called large.php) and measures the time between starting the download and document.ready. It verifies that slower download speed when the firewall rules are in place.

```
<script type="text/javascript">
function networkTest() {
        var bench = new Benchmark();
        bench.start();
        $.ajax({
            url: "large.php",
            success: function() {
                bench.stop();
                alert("Time to download is:" + bench.get());
            }
        });
    }
</script>
```

A Short Note on Load Testing

Load testing is designed to measure the performance of your web server. I would recommend this kind of testing if you have lots of HTTP requests or are expecting lots of traffic. Some shared hosting providers (mentioned in Chapter 1) will limit the number of HTTP requests per second to their servers to avoid server crashes, and so on.

There are many tools for this kind of testing but the one we use is already installed on your Mac and it's called Apache Bench, or ab. So open a terminal and navigate to the Apache home/bin.

Companion Site Reference

Example 13-4: Follow the link below to run this example on the companion site.

http://www.learnhtml5book.com/chapter13/network.php

A sample command looks like this:

```
ab -n 100 -c 10 http://dev.learnhtml5book.com/index.php
```

where –n represents the number of requests, –c represents the number of concurrent connections, and the last parameter is a URL, in this case my development server for this book's companion website.

The output looks like this:

```
Server Software:        Apache/2.2.14
Server Hostname:        dev.learnhtml5book.com
Server Port:            80
Document Path:          /index.php
Document Length:        1732 bytes
Concurrency Level:      10
Time taken for tests:   0.308 seconds
Complete requests:      100
Failed requests:        0
Write errors:           0
Total transferred:      194500 bytes
HTML transferred:       173200 bytes
Requests per second:    324.54 [#/sec] (mean)
Time per request:       30.813 [ms] (mean)
Time per request:       3.081 [ms] (mean, across all concurrent requests)
Transfer rate:          616.43 [Kbytes/sec] received
Connection Times (ms)
              min  mean[+/-sd] median   max
Connect:        1   26  13.0     24      58
Processing:     0    4  11.4      0      40
Waiting:        0    3  10.8      0      40
Total:         14   30  11.0     28      58

Percentage of the requests served within a certain time (ms)
  50%     28
  66%     37
  75%     40
  80%     41
```

```
 90%     43
 95%     52
 98%     56
 99%     58
100%     58 (longest request)
```

The full documentation for Apache Bench (v 2.2) is available from

```
http://httpd.apache.org/docs/2.2/programs/ab.html
```

Performance Test Conclusions

If you notice from Table 13-2 the iOS devices in mobile Safari, the native JavaScript querySelector is much faster than using jQuery. If you are doing a lot of DOM manipulation and performance is a concern you might want to build your own components using these functions as they are on average 30% faster and don't require an additional download of the jQuery library.

Table 13-2. Performance Comparison Revisited

Test	iPad v1 (ms)	iPhone4 (ms)	Chrome v15 (ms)	Safari 5.1.2 (ms)
Simple	13	19	2	2
Native JS	432	541	87	183
jQuery 1.6.4	567	705	83	213

You should test your application's network performance as well as benchmark your site and APIs to see if they are going to be bottlenecks to your overall application performance.

Automated Testing

Testing your application over and over can be quite time consuming. Also as you modify your application, even though you have a unit test you still want to have eyes on your application to know that things are still working from end to end. There is a variety of products and tools out there that can do this but the one I'm most fond of is a library created for the Ruby programming language called Watir (pronounced "water").

Because Ruby is installed out of the box on your Mac there are just a few things you need to do to automate testing through Safari.

▓ **Note** Although there are some native apps and third-party libraries that allow you to test through the iPhone, I've found that I can do about 90% plus of my testing through my desktop browser.

```
sudo gem update-system
sudo gem install rb-appscript
sudo gem install safariwatir
```

Second, you need a page to access and do something for my sample set-up. I use the companion site and create a simple page with a button I can click. The HTML for this is below.

Companion Site Reference

Example 13-5: Follow the link below to run this example on the companion site.

http://www.learnhtml5book.com/chapter13/watir.php

```
<button name="test" onclick="test()">Test Button</button>
<script type="text/javascript">
function test() {
    alert("this is a test alert");
}
</script>
```

Finally, I create a simple test in Ruby that opens Safari, and navigates to this page, and clicks this button:

```
//to run type from the command prompt: ruby script.rb
require 'rubygems'
require 'safariwatir'

browser = Watir::Safari.new
browser.goto("http://dev.learnhtml5book.com")
browser.link(:text, "Chapter 13 - Mobile Testing").click
browser.link(:text, "Watir").click
browser.button(:name, "test").click
```

That's it. You can now automate until your heart's content. To make things even better there's a package that allows you to integrate your BDD test mentioned earlier with your automated testing called Cucumber.

You can find out more about Cucumber at: http://cukes.info/.

■ **Other Testing Tools** This is not the only automated testing tool. There are others like Selenium and Windmill. Just enter a Google search for "automated web testing," browser plugins that will record your steps, or stand-alone proxy tools, but none I would recommend at this time just because I always use Watir.

A/B Testing

The final kind of testing I discuss in this chapter is going to solve the problem of "What do you do when you have two or more designs and you want to measure the conversion or click-through rate?" These AB tests or experiments are often used on websites to measure whether a particular photo or placement of a button gets users to buy something and increase the value of their purchase, or click through to another page.

For our AB test I show you how to use a simple cookie to show content dynamically for your mobile page. First you need to decide what version you want to be represented as A (this is usually your existing site), and what version you want for B (this is usually your test case).

Companion Site Reference

Example 13-6: Follow the link below to run this example on the companion site.

```
http://www.learnhtml5book.com/chapter13/abtest.php
```

In the example below I just use a CSS to hide both of the <div> tags.

```
<style>
    .abtest {
        display: none;
    }
</style>
<div id="a" class="abtest">Usually this is the original version (Version A).</div>
<div id="b" class="abtest">Usually this is the new version (Version B).</div>
```

Next, you need a way to get and set cookies:

```
<script type="text/javascript">
    function getCookie(name) {
        var result = "";
        var start = document.cookie.indexOf(name + "=");
        var end;
        if (start != -1) {
            start += (name.length + 1);
            end = document.cookie.indexOf(";", start);
            if (end == -1)
                end = document.cookie.length;
            result = unescape(document.cookie.substring(start, end));
        }
        return result;
    }

    function setCookie(name, value, expire_days) {
        var expire = new Date();
        expire.setDate(expire.getDate() + expire_days);
        var value = escape(value) + ((expire_days == null) ? "" : "; expires=" +↵
 expire.toUTCString());
        document.cookie = name + "=" + value;
    }
</script>
```

Then you need a way to set a random cookie and then, based on this random cookie, pick which version to show:

```
<script type="text/javascript">
var random = Math.floor(Math.random() * 100) + 1;
```

```
    var abcookie = getCookie("abtest");
    if (abcookie == "") {
        // if greater than 50 set to version 'a' otherwise 'b'
        (random > 50) ? setCookie("abtest", "a", 30) : setCookie("abtest", "b", 30);
    }
    if (abcookie == "a") {
        document.querySelector("#a").style.display = 'inline';
    } else {
        document.querySelector("#b").style.display = 'inline';
    }
</script>
```

If you don't want to roll your own, Google even has a tool for this called Website Optimizer, which you can find out more about at: http://www.google.com/websiteoptimizer.

In addition, you can set these in Google Analytics via custom attributes or append them to your Apache logs so you can get a good measure of performance of each of these cookies as they relate to your site. You can't do that with local storage.

Putting It All Together

I use a lot of GPS in the Grandview Avenue app. One of the common functions I use is to validate GPS coordinates. So I write a GPS validation function for the area in which my app will be active.

First, Create the Test Harness

This is the HTML that will run your test. It contains the Jasmine zip files you downloaded earlier as well as the spec JavaScript file of your new code and the library you've written.

```
<!DOCTYPE HTML PUBLIC "-//W3C//DTD HTML 4.01 Transitional//EN"
        "http://www.w3.org/TR/html4/loose.dtd">
<html>
<head>
    <title>Jasmine Test Runner</title>
    <link rel="stylesheet" type="text/css" href="jasmine/jasmine.css">
    <script type="text/javascript" src="jasmine/jasmine.js"></script>
    <script type="text/javascript" src="jasmine/jasmine-html.js"></script>
    <script type="text/javascript" src="/m/js/grandviewave-mobile.js"></script>
    <!-- include spec files here... -->
    <script type="text/javascript" src="gps-spec.js"></script>
</head>
<body>

<script type="text/javascript">
    jasmine.getEnv().addReporter(new jasmine.TrivialReporter());
    jasmine.getEnv().execute();
</script>
</body>
</html>
```

After you've created this file it does not do much so now we need to write our specification. (You do this first in TDD.)

Second, Create the SPEC

The spec first verifies invalid co-ordinates. Second, it verifies good co-ordinates.

```
describe('getCurrentPosition()', function() {
    it('test for invalid coordinates', function() {
        expect(validateGPS(0, 0)).toBeFalsy();
        expect(validateGPS(39, 83)).toBeFalsy();
        expect(validateGPS(39, -99)).toBeFalsy();
        expect(validateGPS(-100, 100)).toBeFalsy();
    });

    it('returns a set of VALID coordinates', function() {
        expect(validateGPS(39, -83)).toBeTruthy();
    });
});
```

Because we have a failing test, we can write the implementation.

Third, Create the Validation Function

The validator just checks for valid latitude (lat) and longitude (lon). I want to return only a certain grid so in this case I just choose a few co-ordinates for latitude (38 and 41) and longitude (–82 and –84) and validate against those.

```
function validateGPS(lat,lon) {
    if (lat -- 0 || lon -- 0) return false;
    if (lat < 38 || lat > 41)  return false;
    if (lon > -82 || lon < -84)  return false;
    if (!isNaN(lat) && !isNaN(lon)) return true;
    return false;
}
```

Now that you've been able to see a passing test, you're good to go. Just remember as you write your custom classes and functions in your JavaScript code you create good test coverage. This way if something changes you can catch yourself.

Chapter Summary

In this chapter I talked about a number of ways to test your mobile web application.

- TDD and BDD test for unit testing your custom JavaScript

- Performance and load testing to gain a better idea of your application's responsiveness even with simulated slower network speeds

- Means to automate testing and optimize your web app's content

Although this chapter on testing is at the end of the book I highly recommend you think about testing every step of the way. It will make you a better developer and ensure the quality of your code is at its best.

The next chapter is a catch-all chapter, talking about things such as web workers (threads for JavaScript) and web sockets and a lot more things you didn't think you could do with plain old JavaScript.

CHAPTER 14

Advanced Topics

This chapter is pretty much a catch-all for the HTML5 APIs I didn't talk about in much detail in Chapter 2 (HTML5 in short). It touches on some useful technology, but perhaps not technology you'll use in the first version of your mobile web app.

The heart of this chapter is about the communications API of HTML5 with topics including cross-domain communication, server-sent events, and web sockets. This gives you the ability to send and receive messages within your web app without the constant polling that's typically used via setInterval() or setTimeout().

I then talk about multithreading via web workers and the additional management of your history object with some new methods and events.

Cross-Domain Communication

Before HTML5, it was difficult to get a browser to communicate between DOMs on different source URLs, specifically different domains, because of something called the *same origin policy*.

The *same origin policy* was introduced as a security feature as a part of Netscape Navigator 2.0 in March of 1996. The basic concept ensured that only scripts running on pages from within the same domain were allowed to access the objects, methods, and properties of other pages within the same domain. This created a number of problems for web developers trying to add features and create mash-ups, but it was also a good thing because of security. To get around the same origin policy, HTML5 added a document messaging API. Yes, it really did take about 15 years to create a workaround.

Let's start by looking at the options that were open to developers before HTML5.

Before HTML5

Let's say your page is http://www.learnhtml5book.com/index.php. How would the URLs in Table 14-1 react to the same origin policy?

Table 14-1. Same Origin Policy Overview

URL	Success	Reason
http://www.learnhtml5book.com/index2.php	Success	Same site, same domain
https://www.learnhtml5book.com/index2.php	Failure	Different protocol

URL	Success	Reason
`http://www.learnhtml5book.com:8080/page2`	Failure	Different port
`http://www2.learnhtml5book.com/index.php`	Failure	Different subdomain
`http://www.grandviewave.com/index.php`	Failure	Different domain

Although the same origin policy proved inconvenient for web developers trying to create something, it prevented predatory sites from grabbing DOM objects such as your Amazon session cookie and ordering a bunch of things on your account or grabbing other personal information.

Before document messaging, there were three main ways to get around this:

- Subdomains via `document.domain`

- Proxy request via a server-side language

- Including third-party scripts

Let's talk about subdomains first.

document.domain

On both the origin domain and the alternate domain, set the `document.domain` property on each of these pages. This allows both DOMs to share data.

```
document.domain = "learnhtml5book.com";
```

Using a Proxy

If your site is on another hosted server you can create a proxy to these data by requesting them via a server-side call from your own domain. Here's a sample proxy used to access remote resources using PHP.

```php
<?php
$url = "http://www.grandviewave.com/api/remote.php";
$remote_page = file_get_contents($url.'&auth_token=↵
d0803e5ec8aee58801c548c1c0356a94f4dd4c73');
echo $remote_page;
?>
```

This page will take the URL specified via the `$url` variable and output it on your page. So if the page above was `http://yourdomain.com/proxy.php`, the actual HTML displayed would be that of the specified URL.

I've used this method when accessing JSON from third-party sites. It also allows me to cache it, which improves my page's latency (time to load).

Including Scripts from Other Domains

A lot of third-party APIs rely on allowing third-party script access by including remote scripts on the origin domain. The example below is the way Google collects analytics information.

```
<script type="text/javascript">
  var _gaq = _gaq || [];
  _gaq.push(['_setAccount', 'UA-aaaaaaa-x']);
  _gaq.push(['_trackPageview']);

  (function() {
    var ga = document.createElement('script'); ga.type = 'text/javascript';↵
ga.async = true;
    ga.src = ('https:' == document.location.protocol ? 'https://ssl' : 'http://www') +↵
'.google-analytics.com/ga.js';
    var s = document.getElementsByTagName('script')[0]; s.parentNode.insertBefore(ga,↵
s);
  })();
</script>
```

■ **Note** Because PhoneGap uses local files and the file:// protocol, it's not subject to the same origin policy. Read more about this in Chapter 15.

So to get around having to hack your way to a useful web application, HTML5 added the cross-document messaging API.

Document Messaging

The document messaging API has the following method.

`window.postMessage(message)`

The receiver of the message just needs to have an event listener called:

`window.onmessage(event)`

Companion Site Reference

Example 14-1: Follow the link below to run this example on the companion site.

`http://www.learnhtml5book.com/chapter14/messaging.php`

One way to implement this is to use an `<iframe>` to include the contents of a remote DOM. For this example I create a simple HTML file on my domain called `http://www.scottpreston.com/messagetest.html`. When this page's onmessage event fires I alert the contents of the message via the event.data property.

```
<p>This &lt;iframe&gt; is from scottpreston.com.</p>
<p id="msg">Send message!</p>
<script type="text/javascript">
```

```
    window.onmessage = function(e) {
        if (e.origin == "http://dev.learnhtml5book.com" || e.origin ==↵
 "http://www.learnhtml5book.com") {
            alert(e.data);
        }
    };
</script>
```

Next on the origin domain's source file I have a <textarea>, <iframe> and a button to initialize the event. In the postMessage method, I send the contents of the <textarea> along with the domain to which I want to post the message. After clicking the button I get an alert pop-up, executed from the remote domain. I could even read cookies or anything if I decide to put that logic inside the onmessage function.

```
<textarea id="msg_txt" name="msg"></textarea>
<button onclick="send()">Send</button><br>
<iframe src="http://www.scottpreston.com/messagetest.html" height="100" width="300"↵
 id="remote_win"></iframe>
<script type="text/javascript">
    function send() {
        var win = document.querySelector("#remote_win").contentWindow;
        var elt = document.querySelector("#msg_txt");
        win.postMessage(
                elt.value, "http://www.scottpreston.com"
        );
        elt.value = ";
    }
</script>
```

You can use any of these methods to assist in cross-domain messaging or to improve performance, which I've done with a proxy. The onmessage event is used throughout this chapter including something really powerful: server-sent events.

Server-Sent Events

The first kinds of communication we covered in this chapter were from browser to browser across different domains. The second kind of messages I talk about are server-sent events.

These events occur directly from server to browser (client). Previous to this specification a JavaScript would need to poll a server on some interval creating a lot of overhead and unneeded traffic. So rather than polling every one or two seconds for an update you can just open a connection and then when something updates you can send an event.

To implement this you first need some server-side code that sends an event-stream. This example just sends the time ($time variable) every five seconds. See Figure 14-1.

```
<?php
header('Content-Type: text/event-stream');
header('Cache-Control: no-cache');
while (true) {
    $time = time();
    echo "data: ". $time . PHP_EOL;
    echo PHP_EOL;
    ob_flush();
    flush();
```

```
    sleep(5); // wait 5 seconds
}
?>
```

Next, you need to open a connection in the client to the server and a way to update the page contents. Again, just as with document messaging, we use the onmessage event. The remainder of the script just contains a few more events and a specialized append() function to update the innerHTML of the <div>.

___

Companion Site Reference

Example 14-2: Follow the link below to run this example on the companion site.

```
http://www.learnhtml5book.com/chapter14/serverevents.php
```

___

```html
<p>See messages below:</p>
<div id="sse_txt"></div>
<script type="text/javascript">
    var source = new EventSource('sse.php');
    var elt = document.querySelector("#sse_txt");
    source.onopen = function(e) {
        append("opening connection");
    };
    source.onmessage = function(e) {
        append(e.data);
    };
    source.onerror = function(e) {
        append("error");
    };
    function append(txt) {
        elt.innerHTML = elt.innerHTML + txt + "-" + new Date() + " -- <br>";
    }
</script>
```

In the example below I'm receiving an event every five seconds. You can program this to poll a database or use whatever interval you want.

Figure 14-1. *Server-Side Events*

Web Sockets

Another kind of communication between a server and a browser is a web socket, which is a bidirectional protocol that travels over a TCP socket. It's not HTTP, but an entirely different socket-based protocol. This means you can't use Apache to send out data without a custom module or proxy to another server.

If you are looking for a way to implement a chat program or other real-time application where you're constantly sending and receiving data from a server or other users, you might use web sockets over traditional http/web programming.

For a list of server implementations see the following.

```
http://en.wikipedia.org/wiki/Comparison_of_WebSocket_implementations
```

Now even though I'm not going to implement a server solution here I'd like to invoke a current web socket at WebSocket.org. Here just like the other message implementations we write an event handler called onmessage, to take care of the response.

To send a message to the web socket, we simply call the method send with our message as the payload. Additional event handlers (not shown) for a WebSocket include, onopen, onerror, and onclose.

Companion Site Reference

Example 14-3: Follow the link below to run this example on the companion site.

`http://www.learnrhtml5book.com/chapter14/websocket.php`

```
<button onclick="test()">Web Socket Test</button>
<script language="javascript" type="text/javascript">
    var websocket = new WebSocket('ws://echo.websocket.org/');
    function test() {
        websocket.send("This Book Rocks!");
    }

    websocket.onmessage = function(evt) {
        alert('RESPONSE: ' + evt.data);
        websocket.close();
    };
</script>
```

To write your own WebSocket server in PHP use:

`http://code.google.com/p/phpwebsocket/`

To write your own WebSocket server in node use:

`https://github.com/miksago/node-websocket-server`

To write your own WebSocket server in Ruby use:

`https://github.com/igrigorik/em-websocket`

For more information on the Web Socket protocol see

`http://dev.w3.org/html5/websockets/`

Web Workers

Web workers give your JavaScript the ability to multithread. You do this because often times you will want to do things in the background without wanting to interfere with your user interface.

However, because of thread safety, workers do not have access to:

- The DOM
- window object
- document object

However, a worker can still access the following.

- navigator object

- location object
- XMLHttpRequest
- setTimeout/clearTimeout, setInterval/clearInterval functions
- applicationCache

To use a web worker it's as simple as creating a new Worker() object with the source of the JavaScript in the constructor. Then as with the other communication functions mentioned previously, just add an onmessage event to capture data returned from the worker. But to send data to the worker we use the postMessage method. The example below sends nothing.

Companion Site Reference

Example 14-4: Follow the link below to run this example on the companion site.

http://www.learnhtml5book.com/chapter14/webworker.php

```
<button onclick="callWorker()">Worker Example</button><br>
<div>Worker Count: <span id="count"></span></div>
<script type="text/javascript">
    var worker = new Worker("js/worker.js");
    worker.onmessage = function(evt) {
        document.querySelector("#count").innerHTML = evt.data;
    };

    function callWorker() {
        worker.postMessage();
    }
</script>
```

In the worker.js file the role of this function is to loop in a one-second interval and post information back to the original source file; then after five seconds stop.

```
 onmessage = function(event) {
    startMe();
}
var count = 0;
function startMe() {
    self.postMessage(count);
    count++;
    if (count<5)
        setTimeout("startMe()",1000);
}
```

You can also use web workers to load scripts via:

importScripts("js/newscript.js");

Places where you might use a web worker would include:

- Background number crunching

- Working with client-side data such as local or session storage
- Performing some background task such as server-side events, WebSockets, or AJAX

The main things you want to think about when using a worker is something you want to happen without it affecting the user interface.

History Management

Before HTML5 the only way you could access the history would be to set a timer and monitor the location.hash property. This constant polling consumes valuable CPU cycles and can be problematic. The preferred method would be to have an event fire when it changes.

The example below sets a timeout and changes the document.location to change every two seconds; then based on the firing of the event onhashchange, I change the innerHTML of a <div> element.

Companion Site Reference

Example 14-5: Follow the link below to run this example on the companion site.

http://www.learnhtml5book.com/chapter14/history.php

```
<button onclick="changeHash()">Web Socket Test</button>
<div id="something">This is some content...</div>
<script type="text/javascript">
var counter = 0;
function changeHash() {
    document.location = "history.php#"+counter;
    if (counter < 5) setTimeout("changeHash()",2000);
    counter++;
}

window.onhashchange = function() {
    var elt = document.querySelector("#something");
    if (counter == 2) {
        elt.innerHTML = "This us something else completely...";
    }

    if (counter == 4) {
        elt.innerHTML = "Yet, something else you might want to read...";
    }
}
</script>
```

Other things you can do with this include:

- history.length: This returns the number of items in the session history.
- history.state: This returns the current state of the history object.

- `history.go(n)`: This allows you to go in any positive or negative direction in this history.

- `history.back()`: This goes back one in the history (like the back button).

- `history.forward()`: This goes forward one in the history (like the forward button).

- `history.pushState(state, title, url)`: This allows you to set a state into the browser's history.

- `history.replaceState(state, title, url)`: This allows you to replace a state in the browser's history by the URL.

■ **Note** The **state object** is just any object you want to put into the history. This object can be any object you want that is bound to the DOM at the point in history where you happen to be.

Chapter Summary

This chapter was a catch-all chapter that included some details on messaging.

This messaging ranged from how to get around the same origin policy in JavaScript by using the `window.postMessage` method and `window.onmessage` event listener.

But we later found out that the `onmessage` event listener could also be applied to the `EventSource` for web workers for multithreading and for server-side events and web sockets for allowing realtime server-to-browser communication without the need for polling.

If you're implementing some rather intensive background task or are looking to speed up the rendering of your interface, then consider using web workers to perform some of these tasks.

If you want to have direct server-to-browser communication such as with a chat client or maybe an interactive GPS-related app, maybe you can use server-side events or web sockets.

This concludes just about everything you can think of doing with Mobile Safari and JavaScript and HTML5. But there's still more to do and that's to take all you've learned and turn it into a Native App via PhoneGap, and that's what we talk about next.

CHAPTER 15

Going Native with PhoneGap

You can do a lot with Mobile Safari, but there's always room for improvement. In particular you might want native controls or even want to take video or photos using your camera, but you can't do that with Mobile Safari. Enter PhoneGap.

PhoneGap was created at an iPhoneDevCamp in San Francisco in 2005.

I started using PhoneGap a few years ago and was amazed at how by just using JavaScript I could access all the basic functions I needed without knowing Objective-C. Basically PhoneGap renders your app using what's called a *UIWebView*. This allows a native app to basically render local HTML, CSS, and JavaScript files in a window using Mobile Safari while allowing access to all the native functions you can't normally access.

Because you're going to create a native app you'll need Xcode. You might find it a larger learning curve to understand Xcode (Apple's Integrated Development Environment) than to understand PhoneGap. Once you build your first app you will be amazed at how simple it is!

For this chapter you probably won't need your trusty browser or the companion site (unless you just want to download the sample app). In fact it might be helpful to download it at the beginning so you can follow along, but first you need to install Xcode and PhoneGap.

Installing PhoneGap

To start using PhoneGap you need an Intel-based Mac with OSX 10.6 or greater.

Next you need to install Xcode from the Apple Developer Portal: `http://developer.apple.com`.

Third you need to download and install PhoneGap from `http://phonegap.com`. This is a .zip file you need to open. After you download the file navigate to iOS and double click the `.dmg`. You should see the installer shown in Figure 15-1.

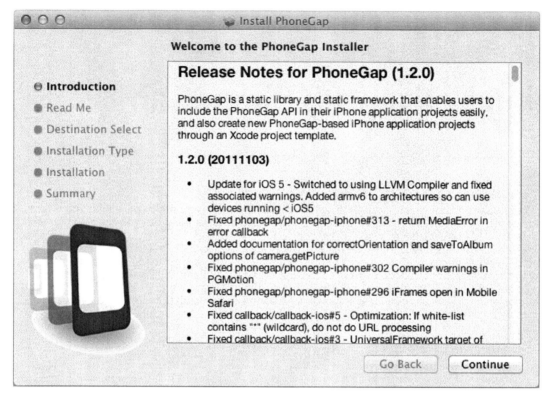

Figure 15-1. Installing the .dmg

Once you install the disk image you are ready to start with your first PhoneGap application. So just open Xcode then select a PhoneGap-based application (see Figure 15-2).

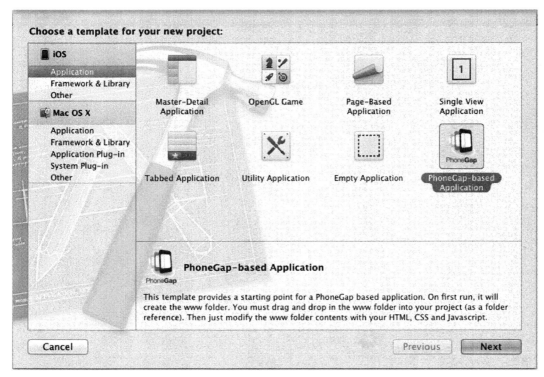

Figure 15-2. *Phone Gap Project Type*

After your project opens just click run and you should see your PhoneGap application open an iPhone simulator with an alert message. The output just displays a simple alert letting you know the event fired (Figure 15-3).

Figure 15-3. Plumbing Test App

■ **Note** I had a problem the first time running. It said it could not find the folder www. To fix this make sure you run PhoneGap at least once and it builds. Then import this project into PhoneGap and ensure you select Copy files.

If you look at the source code for your first app you will see there's not much to it, just some formatting for the viewport in the <meta> tag and a custom event listener called "deviceready". That's it.

```
<!DOCTYPE html>
<html>
<head>
<title></title>
<meta name="viewport" content="width=device-width, initial-scale=1.0, maximum-scale=↵
1.0, user-scalable=no;" />
```

```
meta charset="utf-8">
script type="text/javascript" charset="utf-8" src="phonegap-1.2.0.js"></script>
<script type="text/javascript">
    function onBodyLoad(){
        document.addEventListener("deviceready", onDeviceReady, false);
    }
    function onDeviceReady() {
        navigator.notification.alert("PhoneGap is working")
    }
</script>
</head>
<body onload="onBodyLoad()">
<h1>Phone Gap Test</h1>
</body></html>
```

Take some time to look around and experiment with your app.

Enhancing Your App

Next you want to enhance your PhoneGap app to do some of the things your mobile app can do and some of the things it can't do, such as access your phone's camera.

▓ **Note** You might want to target your iPhone or iPad device when you try these as the simulator might give you errors.

Geolocation

PhoneGap uses the same objects as Mobile Safari; there's no need to change any syntax as PhoneGap just overrides these functions to call native code.

```
function testGeo(         {
navigator.geolocation.getCurrentPosition(geoSuccess, allError);
}

function geoSuccess(position) {
    alert('Latitude: ' + position.coords.latitude + '\n' +
            'Longitude: ' + position.coords.longitude + '\n' +
            'Altitude: ' + position.coords.altitude + '\n' +
            'Accuracy: ' + position.coords.accuracy + '\n' +
            'Altitude Accuracy: ' + position.coords.altitudeAccuracy + '\n' +
            'Heading: ' + position.coords.heading + '\n' +
            'Speed: ' + position.coords.speed + '\n' +
            'Timestamp: ' + new Date(position.timestamp) + '\n');
}
```

233

Accelerometer

Again as with geolocation you can either use built-in Safari functions discussed in Chapter 11 or you can use the PhoneGap object. Here are the two examples side by side.

```
//mobile web
window.ondevicemotion = function(evt) {
    accelSuccess(evt.acceleration);
};

// phonegap
function testAccel() {
        navigator.accelerometer.getCurrentAcceleration(accelSuccess, allError);
}

function accelSuccess(acceleration) {
        alert('Acceleration X: ' + acceleration.x + '\n' +
                'Acceleration Y: ' + acceleration.y + '\n' +
                'Acceleration Z: ' + acceleration.z + '\n' +
                'Timestamp: '       + acceleration.timestamp + '\n');
}
```

Vibrate or Beep

Making the phone vibrate is something you can't do in Mobile Safari. You can also make your phone beep.

```
function vibrate() {
     navigator.notification.vibrate(2000); //milliseconds
     navigator.notification.beep(2); // numbr of times
}
```

You can use this to notify a user when a message arrives, for feedback during a game, or maybe even to provide an audio cue to do something else.

Using the Camera

So finally you can access your camera using JavaScript. Just call the getPicture method and you can return data in a Base64 encoded string for rendering in the UIWebView of PhoneGap.

```
function testCamera() {
    clearPhoto();
    navigator.camera.getPicture(camSuccess, allError, { quality: 50 });
}

function camSuccess(imageData) {
   var image = document.querySelector('#myImage');
   image.src = "data:image/jpeg;base64," + imageData;
}

function clearPhoto() {
    var image = document.querySelector('#myImage');
    image.src = "";
}
```

There are a few things you can do with a camera in your application. Although designing a photo-editing application might be a little bit heavy in terms of processing, you could do it with some of the examples from Chapter 9, "Canvas."

Augmented reality apps might also be a little heavy in terms of processing but you could create a game where you tag locations of various things and upload them to a server for further processing.

Or how about interacting with the camera to augment an existing content management system? Imagine taking pictures for your blog or CMS right from the same device on which you're entering your text? That could be your next app!

PhoneGap API Overview

The PhoneGap API is the complete API that's installed by default after you install PhoneGap. So out of the box you can do quite a bit, all with a little JavaScript.

I go over a short summary of the API below along with some methods and properties of these objects as this could give you a taste of what's possible with a little JavaScript and a powerful native library (PhoneGap).

Accelerometer

This allows you to capture motion in the x-, y-, and z-directions. You can use the accelerometer object with PhoneGap or use native Safari.

- `accelerometer.getCurrentAcceleration`
- `accelerometer.watchAcceleration`
- `accelerometer.clearWatch`

Camera

This object gives you the ability to interact with your phone's camera. There are options to save your photo to your photo library, or an album. The image is returned as a Base64 encoded string, however, you can still save locally and then use a method to return a string of the file's location for future processing.

To implement just pass a few functions and a set of options to the method.

- `camera.getPicture`

Capture

These give you the ability to capture audio, images, and video from your device.

- `capture.captureAudio`
- `capture.captureImage`
- `capture.captureVideo`
- `MediaFile.getFormatData`

Compass

These allow you to capture compass-related data via the PhoneGap object versus native.

- `compass.getCurrentHeading`

235

- compass.watchHeading
- compass.clearWatch
- compass.watchHeadingFilter
- compass.clearWatchFilter

Connection

This is a property that allows you to test the connection type: either WiFi, 2G, 3G, 4G, or NONE.

- connection.type

Contacts

These provide access to the contacts database.

- contacts.create
- contacts.find

Device

This gives you the ability to read information on the device such as name, platform, UUID, and version, among others.

Events

These give you the ability to interact with other parts of the device.

- deviceready
- pause
- resume
- online
- offline
- backbutton
- batterycritical
- batterylow
- batterystatus
- menubutton
- searchbutton
- startcallbutton
- endcallbutton
- volumedownbutton
- volumeupbutton

File Objects

These give you the ability to interact with the device file system.

- DirectoryEntry
- DirectoryReader
- File
- FileEntry
- FileError
- FileReader
- FileSystem
- FileTransfer
- FileTransferError
- FileUploadOptions
- FileUploadResult
- FileWriter
- Flags
- LocalFileSystem
- Metadata

Geolocation

These give access to the GPS on your device.

- geolocation.getCurrentPosition
- geolocation.watchPosition
- geolocation.clearWatch

Media

These give the ability to record or play back media on the device.

- media.getCurrentPosition
- media.getDuration
- media.play
- media.pause
- media.release
- media.seekTo
- media.startRecord
- media.stopRecord
- media.stop

Notification

These give you the ability to access the native notification mechanism, specifically beep and vibrate.

- `notification.alert`
- `notification.confirm`
- `notification.beep`
- `notification.vibrate`

Storage

This function utilizes WebSQL databases. I've not talked about these databases as they are deprecated and are no longer active.

- `openDatabase`

Plugins

Outside of the standard APIs discussed above there are a number of third-party plugins to PhoneGap. These plugins give you the ability to do much more, such as iAds, NativeControls, or Google Analytics.

For a complete list of plugins please visit GitHub:

`https://github.com/phonegap/phonegap-plugins`

A Plugin Example—NativeControls

One of the features you might want to add to your PhoneGap app is native controls for features such as tabbed navigation. This involves downloading the control from the plugin site and placing the `.h` and `.m` files in the Plugins folder in Xcode, and the `.js` file in your `/www` directory.

You also need to ensure that you update your `PhoneGap.plist` (Figure 15-4) because this tells your project to which plugins it has access. I added a `NativeControls` key-value pair.

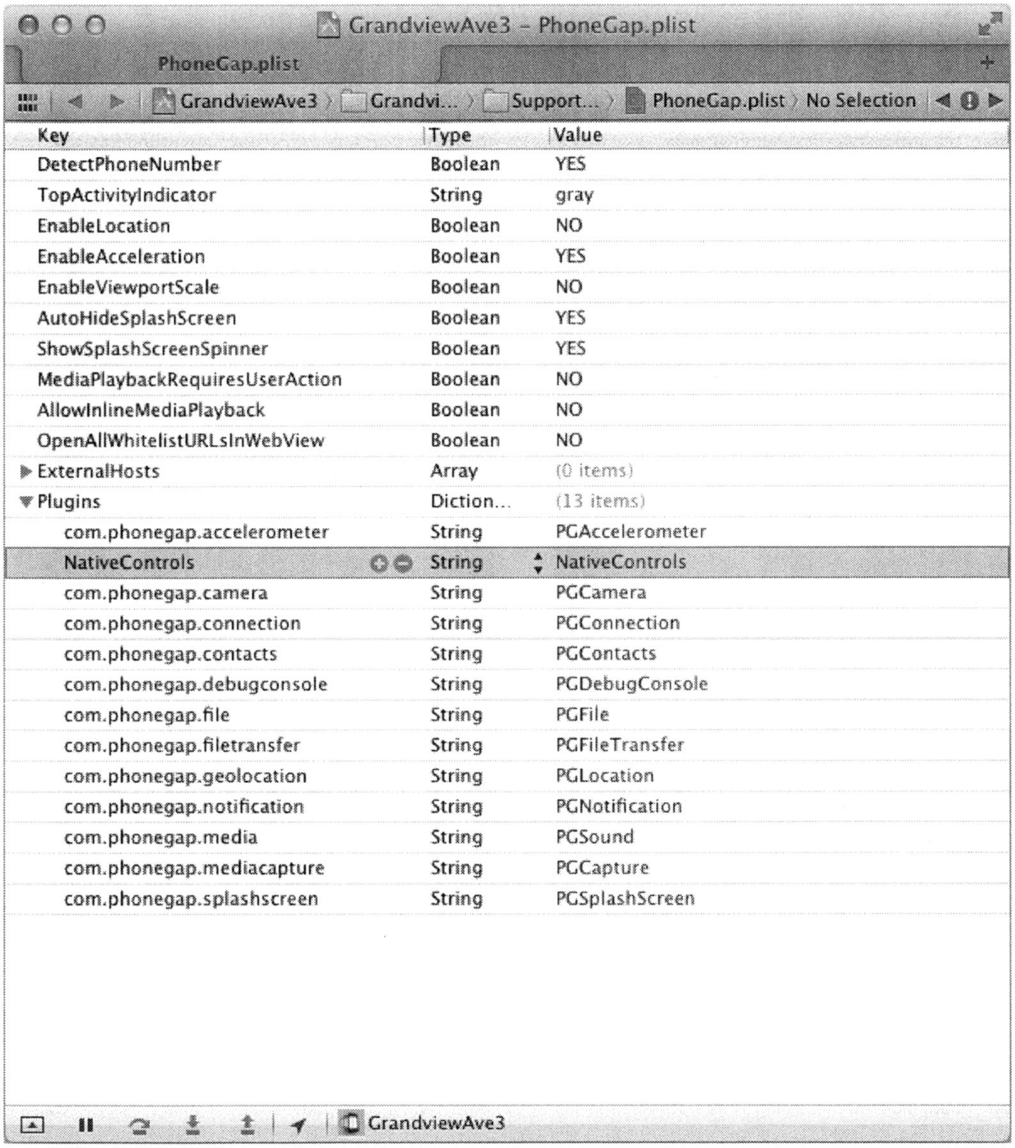

Figure 15-4. PhoneGap.plist

After adding this all you need to do is clean and build from the Product Menu in Xcode. Just be sure to include your NativeControls.js file like so:

```
<script type="text/javascript" charset="utf-8" src="js/phonegap-1.2.0.js"></script>
<script type="text/javascript" charset="utf-8" src="js/NativeControls.js"></script>
```

Your directory structure might look something like Figure 15.5 with your NativeControls.h and NativeControls.m files in the Plugins directory and your JavaScript file in /www/js.

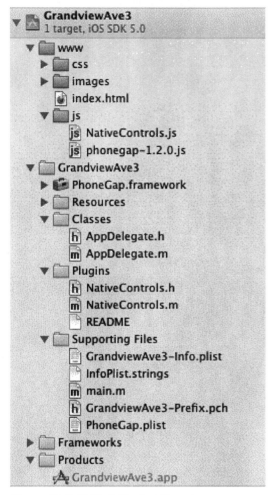

Figure 15-5. X-Code Project Structure

■ **Note** Create your /www directory just as you would your mobile directory; put your CSS, images, and js files in separate folders for better organization.

To access the functionality of the native controls you just need to call the methods on the NativeControls object you've added.

I create a global variable called nativeControls so I can access and update this object later; then inside loadTabs() I create the tab bar, then start creating the tabs one by one. Finally, I set the location and order of the tabs as well as the default-selected tab.

▓ **Note** Don't be confused by the case of the object name; it can be anything you want.

```
var nativeControls;
function loadTabs() {
  nativeControls = new NativeControls();
  nativeControls.createTabBar();
  nativeControls.createTabBarItem("tab1","The Ave", "www/images/city.png",↵
{onSelect : function() {}});
  nativeControls.createTabBarItem("tab2","Near Me", "www/images/location.png",↵
{onSelect : function()
    {}});
  nativeControls.createTabBarItem("tab3","Specials", "www/images/tag.png",↵
{onSelect : function() {}});
  nativeControls.createTabBarItem("tab4","Parking", "www/images/parking.png",↵
{onSelect : function()
    {}});
  nativeControls.createTabBarItem("tab5","More", "tabButton:More", {onSelect :↵
function() {}});
  nativeControls.showTabBar("bottom");
  nativeControls.showTabBarItems("tab1","tab2","tab3","tab4", "tab5");
  nativeControls.selectTabBarItem("tab1");
}
```

After you compile and build you see the native controls at the bottom of your screen (see Figure 15-6).

Figure 15-6. Sample Tabs Using Native Controls

If you want to learn more about PhoneGap online the http://phonegap.com is a great resource!
If you want to learn more about PhoneGap plugins, you can download them from:
https://github.com/phonegap/phonegap-plugins.

Mobile Web App Versus Native App

So far we've talked about some of the ways PhoneGap can help you enhance your app, and we've seen some more of PhoneGap's features in overview. To put all this in context and to sum up why you should take this final step with your app, I've put a little chart together in Table 15-1 to compare and contrast the mobile web, PhoneGap, and Native apps.

Table 15-1. *App Comparison*

	Mobile Web	PhoneGap	Native
Network Access	Yes	Yes	Yes
Display Web Content	Yes	Yes	Yes
Performance	Good	Better	Best
Graphics	HTML5	HTML5	Full 3D GL
Hardware Access	Accelerometer, Gyroscope, Compass, GPS	Accelerometer, Gyroscope, Compass, GPS, Camera	Full
Native Controls	No	Limited	Yes
File	No	Yes	Yes

One last time, let's see what happens when we put it all together.

Putting It All Together

We already have a mobile site, but now it's time to take everything we've done and adapt it to a Native App. The first thing we do is add a splash screen.

In Xcode there is a Resources directory off the main project folder, and two subfolders: icons and splash. Your icons will be 57 × 57 pixels and 114 × 114 pixels for the `icon@2x.png` file, and your splash screens will be 480 × 320 and 960 × 640 for the `Default@2x.png`. By just overwriting the default files then cleaning and rebuilding your app, you will get your icon and splash screen set.

Figure 15-7. Grandview Avenue Mobile App Splash

This splash (Figure 15-7) will show for a few seconds then it will take you to your home page (index.html).

The Home Page

The page that's loaded after the splash will be index.html.

This page is just an HTML page using jQuery Mobile mainly for the effects and styling. The sequence of loading is the CSS, followed by PhoneGap libraries, PhoneGap plugins, jQuery core, and Mobile, followed by application-specific code in grandviewave.js.

Next up is some standard jQuery mobile mark-up.

```
<!DOCTYPE html>
<html>
<head>
  <title></title>
  <meta name="viewport" content="width=device-width, initial-scale=1.0,↵
```

```
maximum-scale=1.0, user-
    scalable=no;" />
  <meta charset="utf-8">
  <link rel="stylesheet" href="css/jquery.mobile-1.0.min.css" />
  <script type="text/javascript" charset="utf-8" src="js/phonegap-1.2.0.js"></script>
  <script type="text/javascript" charset="utf-8" src="js/NativeControls.js"></script>
  <script type="text/javascript" charset="utf-8" src="js/jquery-1.6.4.min.js"></script>
  <script type="text/javascript" charset="utf-8" src="js/jquery↩
.mobile-1.0.min.js"></script>
  <script type="text/javascript" charset="utf-8" src="js/grandviewave.js"></script>
</head>
<body onload="onBodyLoad()">
  <div data-role="page" data-theme="a" id="home">
  <div data-role="header">
  <div class="header1">
  <img src="images/logo.png" alt="gave.com" />
  </div>
  </div>
  <div data-role="content">
  <img src="images/grandviewave.jpg" style="border-radius:8px;width:280px;">
  <ul data-role="listview" data-inset="true" data-theme="c" data-dividertheme="a">
  <li><a href="bizdir.php">Business Directory</a></li>
  </ul>
  </div>
 </div>
</body>
</html>
```

▦ **Note** I've also not included every data-role="page" in the code above but the application will have one of these for each of the pages/screens the user will visit.

You can see from the screen capture of the home page in Figure 15-8 that it's very close to the mobile site, but rather than using the jQuery Mobile tabs, I have native looking tabs at the bottom of the app.

Figure 15-8. Grandview Avenue—Start Screen

In order to access the data from www.grandviewave.com, I just use AJAX to load the content into page elements, some of which I preload and cache in sessionStorage when the app starts up.

To see how I preload all the content from my API I have the following function I call onLoad().

The base_url is my API URL consisting of http://sitename/directory/. And because I can update the content on my server dynamically, I don't need to publish a new app each time I want to update the database.

```
function loadPages() {
  $.get(base_url + 'cats.php', function(data) {
  sessionStorage.put("category_data",data);
    $("#cats").html(data);
  });
  $.get(base_url + 'specials.php', function(data) {
  sessionStorage.put("special_data",data);
    $('#specials_info').html(data);
  });
}
```

Finally to make my navigation a little more native I use the custom controls such as this for my specials tab.

```
nativeControls.createTabBarItem("tab3","Specials", "www/images/tag.png", {
  onSelect : function() {
    $.mobile.changePage("#specials", "pop");
  }
});
```

This would cause the tab to change the page to #specials (a hidden <div> with an id="specials") via the pop transition.

Publishing to the App Store

There are several steps you need to follow to publish an app to the App Store. On a high level, you need to do the following.

1. Create a developer account.

2. Create a certificate signing request .

3. Download a certificate.

4. Create a provisioning profile (developer and for distribution on App Store).

5. Add an AppID (this links your binary file via Info.plist of your app with your provisioning profile at Apple.

6. Build your app for distribution.

7. Submit your app as a Zip file via iTunesConnect.

8. Wait for approval (up to a week).

For more information on publishing to the App Store please follow the detailed information on the Apple Developer website. There's a lot of information there and there are many steps to follow.

```
https://developer.apple.com/ios/manage/distribution/index.action
```

If you don't want to submit via the App Store and would rather just install your app to a handful of devices you just need to create a developer provisioning profile.

Also, when submitting to the App Store it's important to keep in mind performance and iOS human interface guidelines. I've personally not had any issues using jQuery mobile and PhoneGap, but please take some time to review this link:

```
https://developer.apple.com/appstore/guidelines.html
```

You should also take some screenshots of your app so you can submit it to the App Store. If your app is a paid app make sure you have the proper banking and financial steps in place; if it's free you can just submit the app with nothing to worry about financially.

Finally when submitting your app, be sure to include links to your website and make sure you have a way for users to contact you in case of any bugs or if they have any questions.

Once your app goes live, make sure to send a link to all your friends so they can download the app and give it a high rating. This will ensure others will try it out!

Chapter Summary

In this chapter we installed PhoneGap and used it to convert our mobile app to a native app. This allows us to make use of native controls for a snappier response to user input and better aesthetics.

This concludes all of the work of building a Mobile Web application or iOS app. As you can see there are many differences between the apps discussed in this and previous chapters and a traditional web application, but there's also a lot of overlap. Some parting advice I'd give to anyone creating something:

"Ship First, Refine Second."

So many times developers "gold-plate": they get to a point where they think something is done and they are ready to ship, then a little doubt creeps in and they add a little bit more, then a little bit more, and then a little bit more. You will have plenty of time to perfect your craft and enhance your product. Don't try to be perfect with version #1.

If you have any questions about the subjects in this book, please feel free to contact me via http://www.learnhtml5book.com. You can also follow me on twitter via @scottpreston. I'll do my best to throw out tips and future code examples using the #learnhtml5book hash tag.

Have Fun!

APPENDIX

Companion Site References

Overview of Companion Site

The companion website www.learnhtml5book.com is designed so you can view examples as you navigate this book and start building your own mobile web app. You can either click along on your iOS device or via Safari or Chrome.

Chapter 1 – Getting Started

The goal of this chapter is to get your project started and cover some of the basics you'll need in the later chapters.

Example 1-1 Redirecting

Ways you can redirect users to your mobile site. Examples include JavaScript and Apache-level redirects.

```
http://www.learnhtml5book.com/chapter1/redirect.php
```

Example 1-2 Full Screen Mode

Viewing a page without the <meta> viewport attribute.

```
http://www.learnhtml5book.com/chapter1/fullscreen.php
```

Example 1-3 Viewport Mode

The same page with the <meta> viewport attribute.

```
http://www.learnhtml5book.com/chapter1/viewport.php
```

Example 1-4 Sample Mobile App Home Page

A sample Grandview Avenue Home page.

```
http://www.learnhtml5book.com/chapter1/samplehome.php
```

Chapter 2 – HTML5 In Short

This chapter is a short overview or quick-reference guide to HTML5 .

Example 2-1 Canvas

Demonstrates `<canvas>`, one of the new elements of HTML5.

`http://www.learnhtml5book.com/chapter2/canvas.php`

Example 2-2 Video

Video taken from Grandview Avenue.

`http://www.learnhtml5book.com/chapter2/video.php`

Example 2-3 Simple Edit

A sample editable `<div>`.

`http://www.learnhtml5book.com/chapter2/edits.php`

Example 2-4 Structural Elements

Shows you how you might use some of the new structural elements like `<header>` or `<footer>`.

`http://www.learnhtml5book.com/chapter2/structure.php`

Example 2-5 Form Example

A sampling of the new `<form>` fields and attributes.

`http://www.learnhtml5book.com/chapter2/form.php`

Putting It All Together

In this section I show you how to format a basic mobile site using the new HTML5 structural elements.

`http://learnhtml5book.com/chapter2/pag1.php`

    I also demonstrate a sample contact form using validation.

`http://learnhtml5book.com/chapter2/pag2.php`

Chapter 3 – CSS3 and iOS Styling

This chapter shows you how to style your iOS mobile web app from scratch, using CSS3 to make it look like a native app. It also shows you some of the newer features of CSS3 and provides an overview of the subject.

Example 3-1 CSS Linked

Load times using a linked style sheet. (Remember to use your web developer tools to view load times.)

`http://www.learnhtml5book.com/chapter3/basics1.php`

Example 3-2 CSS Imported

Load times using the @import to bring in a style sheet. (Remember to use your web developer tools to view load times.)

`http://www.learnhtml5book.com/chapter3/basics2.php`

Example 3-3 Orientation Selection

How to detect for orientation via CSS.

`http://www.learnhtml5book.com/chapter3/orient.php`

Example 3-4 iOS Selector

How to select for different iOS devices using CSS.

`http://www.learnhtml5book.com/chapter3/iosselect.php`

Example 3-5 Retina Sample

Two images—one optimized for the Retina display.

`http://www.learnhtml5book.com/chapter3/retina.php`

Example 3-6 Sample Header

A sample iOS-styled header.

`http://www.learnhtml5book.com/chapter3/sample_header.php`

Example 3-7 Sample Simple Style

A sample list showing basic styling.

`http://www.learnhtml5book.com/chapter3/sample_list.php`

Example 3-8 Sample iPhone Style

The same list as the previous example but with some iOS styling enhancements.

`http://www.learnhtml5book.com/chapter3/sample_list2.php`

Example 3-9 Sample Buttons

Sample iOS–styled buttons using CSS3.

`http://www.learnhtml5book.com/chapter3/sample_buttons.php`

Example 3-10 iPad Sample

Sample navigation using CSS for the iPad.

`http://www.learnhtml5book.com/chapter3/ipad.php`

Putting It All Together

Elements of this chapter are used throughout the Grandview Avenue mobile site.

Chapter 4 – JavaScript and APIs

The goal of this chapter is to provide an overview of JavaScript and include a number of examples using both classic Ajax and jQuery Ajax to give you a feel for how to do something without a mobile framework.

Example 4-1 First Class Functions

First Class Functions in the JavaScript language.

`http://www.learnhtml5book.com/chapter4/jsfunction.php`

Example 4-2 JavaScript Objects

Object-oriented JavaScript.

`http://www.learnhtml5book.com/chapter4/objects.php`

Example 4-3 Load Events

Load times of two "load" events.

`http://www.learnhtml5book.com/chapter4/load.php`

Example 4-4 Events Sample

Using the onOrientationChange event. This gives you an alternative to using the CSS3 media queries in Chapter 3.

http://www.learnhtml5book.com/chapter4/orient.php

Example 4-5 Dialogs

How to use the different dialog options.

http://www.learnhtml5book.com/chapter4/dialog.php

Example 4-6 Console Logs

Different console logs.

http://www.learnhtml5book.com/chapter4/console.php

Example 4-7 Ajax

An Ajax request using the XMLHttpRequest object (Old-School).

http://www.learnhtml5book.com/chapter4/ajax.php

Example 4-8 JSON

A JSON example.

http://www.learnhtml5book.com/chapter4/json.php

Example 4-9 Ajax Example #1

Classic Ajax example with JSON loads data on a screen.

http://www.learnhtml5book.com/chapter4/combo.php

Example 4-10 Creating Elements

How to create DOM elements.

http://www.learnhtml5book.com/chapter4/creating.php

Example 4-11 Simple jQuery

An overview of using the jQuery ready() event to create an alert().

http://www.learnhtml5book.com/chapter4/jquery.php

Putting It All Together

Elements of this chapter are used throughout the Grandview Avenue mobile site. Two examples are included on the companion site.

Content-loading example using jQuery with a fade-in effect.

`http://www.learnhtml5book.com/chapter4/about.php`

An Ajax example with JSON and jQuery.

`http://www.learnhtml5book.com/chapter4/cats.php`

Chapter 5 – Mobile Frameworks

The goal of this chapter is to provide you an overview of the various benefits of using a mobile web framework versus doing everything manually.

Example 5-1 Using the iUI

A sample page showing the iUI framework—an alternative to jQuery Mobile.

`http://www.learnhtml5book.com/chapter5/iui/index.html`

Example 5-2 Using jQuery Mobile (JQM)

A sample page using the jQuery Mobile framework.

`http://www.learnhtml5book.com/chapter5/jquerymobile/index.html`

Example 5-3 JQM Headers

A sample jQuery Mobile header with buttons.

`http://www.learnhtml5book.com/chapter5/jquerymobile/headers.html`

Example 5-4 JQM Multiple Pages

A multi-page template that uses jQuery mobile.

`http://www.learnhtml5book.com/chapter5/jquerymobile/twopage.html`

Example 5-5 JQM Buttons

A variety of buttons you can use in jQuery Mobile.

`http://www.learnhtml5book.com/chapter5/jquerymobile/buttons.html`

Example 5-6 JQM List

A variety of lists you can use in jQuery Mobile.

`http://www.learnhtml5book.com/chapter5/jquerymobile/lists.html`

Putting It All Together

I've chosen to use the jQuery mobile framework for the Grandview Avenue Mobile Web App. Although it's not perfect it does most of what I want from a styling perspective.

Chapter 6 – Usability, Navigation, and Touch

The goal of this chapter is to highlight various means of navigating your mobile site, touch on some usability concerns, and summarize some events related to a touch versus a click interface.

Example 6-1 JQM Drill Down #1

How to implement a traditional drill-down navigation metaphor using jQuery Mobile.

`http://www.learnhtml5book.com/chapter6/drill1.php`

Example 6-2 JQM Drill Down #2

This is the same example as the previous one, but this time it has a different header with a back button.

`http://www.learnhtml5book.com/chapter6/drill2.php`

Example 6-3 JQM Tabbed Footers

How to implement a tabbed footer navigation using jQuery Mobile.

`http://www.learnhtml5book.com/chapter6/tabs.php`

Example 6-4 JQM Modal Dialogs

How to use modal dialogs using jQuery Mobile.

`http://www.learnhtml5book.com/chapter6/modals.php`

Example 6-5 JQM Events #1

How to use the various supported events in jQuery mobile like swipe and touch.

`http://www.learnhtml5book.com/chapter6/events.php`

Example 6-6 JQM Events #2

How to do the same thing as the previous example but manually with JavaScript.

`http://www.learnhtml5book.com/chapter6/events2.php`

Putting It All Together

In this section I decided on a navigation metaphor for the mobile site and created a sample iPad left navigation.

Chapter 7 – GPS and Google Maps

The goal of this chapter is to show you how to interact with the GPS sensor in your phone and integrate that sensor with Google Maps.

Example 7-1 GPS Basics

How to get the GPS coordinates from your device.

`http://www.learnhtml5book.com/chapter7/basics.php`

Example 7-2 Google Maps Basics

How to create a basic Google Map using a little HTML and JavaScript.

`http://www.learnhtml5book.com/chapter7/gmap.php`

Example 7-3 Google Maps Geocoding

How to place a marker and use geocoding to turn an address into a set of GPS coordinates.

`http://www.learnhtml5book.com/chapter7/gmap2.php`

Example 7-4 Static Google Maps

How to do the same thing as the previous example but with a URL versus JavaScript.

`http://www.learnhtml5book.com/chapter7/static.php`

Example 7-5 Current Location Map

Combines getting GPS coordinates from your device and interacting via Google Maps.

`http://www.learnhtml5book.com/chapter7/currentlocation.php`

Putting It All Together

For Grandview Avenue I use a lot of Google Maps and GPS. Each business has a GPS location as well as parking locations. I've combined all of these to provide some awesome functionality on the mobile website.

Chapter 8 – Animation and Effects

The main goal of this chapter is to show you how to manually create some effects and animation with your CSS and a little JavaScript. Most of the time a framework or plug-in might do this for you, but often it's easier and requires less code to write it yourself.

Example 8-1 CSS Tricks

There are three examples here. Two show sample gradients and one shows reflection of an element.

```
http://www.learnhtml5book.com/chapter8/tricks.php
```

Example 8-2 Transitions

The transition between two different CSS states via hover.

```
http://www.learnhtml5book.com/chapter8/transitions.php
```

Example 8-3 Transforms

Rotations, zooms, and some examples of 3D transforms.

```
http://www.learnhtml5book.com/chapter8/transforms.php
```

Example 8-4 Animations

Four sample animations done through key frames, which start automatically.

```
http://www.learnhtml5book.com/chapter8/animations.php
```

Example 8-5 Adding JavaScript

How to automatically invoke transitions, transforms, and animations via JavaScript.

```
http://www.learnhtml5book.com/chapter8/addingjs.php
```

Putting It All Together

I use some CSS tricks from this chapter in the Grandview Ave app. These were done automatically via jQuery Mobile and a 2D Transition that provides a "Zoom" feature for the website's business profile detail page.

Chapter 9 – Canvas

This chapter shows you the various ways you can use the `<canvas>` element.

Example 9-1 Drawing Stuff

How to draw shapes like circles, squares, triangles, and text.

`http://www.learnhtml5book.com/chapter9/drawing.php`

Example 9-2 Interacting

Drawing on the canvas based on an ontouch event.

`http://www.learnhtml5book.com/chapter9/interact.php`

Example 9-3 Images

How to load images, do some image processing by converting an image to grayscale, and then add a slider to create a threshold filter effect on the image.

`http://www.learnhtml5book.com/chapter9/images.php`

Example 9-4 Animation

How to animate an image using `<canvas>`.

`http://www.learnhtml5book.com/chapter9/animation.php`

Putting It All Together

In this section, I decided to modify the Sales & Specials from an ordinary list to a game utilizing the slot machine code from the animation example. You can view this by going to `http://grandviewave.com/m` and clicking on Sales.

Chapter 10 – Audio and Video

This chapter touches on how to use the audio and video elements of HTML5.

Example 10-1 Audio Example

How to use the audio element.

`http://www.learnhtml5book.com/chapter10/audio.php`

Example 10-2 Video Example

How to use the video element.

`http://www.learnhtml5book.com/chapter10/video.php`

Putting It All Together

I decided to create audio and video tours of Grandview Avenue and integrate these tours with GPS. View these on http://grandviewave.com/m.

Chapter 11 – Native Services

This chapter shows you how to integrate with some of the other features on your iOS device like the compass, gyroscope, accelerometer, and even interact with native apps from your mobile web app.

Example 11-1 Orientation

How to use the orientation sensor to get readings from the compass and the device's orientation in space.

`http://www.learnhtml5book.com/chapter11/orientation.php`

▨ **Note** This even works on your Mac-Book Pro with Google Chrome.

Example 11-2 Motion

How to use the accelerometer in your iOS device to detect motion.

`http://www.learnhtml5book.com/chapter11/motion.php`

Example 11-3 Links

How to use custom links to integrate with other apps already installed on your iOS device.

`http://www.learnhtml5book.com/chapter11/links.php`

Putting It All Together

I decided to use the orientation feature to create an "Easter egg" in the Grandview Avenue mobile site. If you happen to be in a certain place, you'll get an interactive panorama augmented reality treat. You're unlikely to be in the right place as you read this book, so go ahead and grab this code to build your own. Make sure you view it in your editor.

`http://learnhtml5book.com/chapter11/pag1.html`

Chapter 12 – Offline Apps and Storage

This chapter shows you various means for taking your application offline and adding storage to your mobile web app.

Example 12-1 Application Manifest

How to allow your sites to work in offline mode (without a network).

`http://www.learnhtml5book.com/chapter12/manifest.php`

Example 12-2 Cookies

How to set and retrieve cookies using JavaScript.

`http://www.learnhtml5book.com/chapter12/cookies.php`

Example 12-3 Local Storage

How to set and retrieve items from `LocalStorage`.

`http://www.learnhtml5book.com/chapter12/local.php`

Example 12-4 Session Storage

How to set and retrieve items from `SessionStorage`.

`http://www.learnhtml5book.com/chapter12/session.php`

Putting It All Together

In this chapter I decided to use `SessionStorage` to improve the web application's performance.

Chapter 13 – Mobile Testing

This chapter introduces you to the different kinds of testing you can do with your mobile web app.

Example 13-1 Test Driven Development

This simple JavaScript shows you how to dive into Test Driven Development (TDD).

`http://www.learnhtml5book.com/chapter13/tdd.php`

Example 13-2 Jasmine

How to extend your TDD with BDD and Jasmine for JavaScript Unit Testing.

`http://www.learnhtml5book.com/chapter13/jasmine.php`

Example 13-3 Benchmarking

How to benchmark your APIs using some DOM manipulation versus pure JavaScript & jQuery.

`http://www.learnhtml5book.com/chapter13/benchmark.php`

Example 13-4 Network Testing

How to test the speed of your download with a simple JavaScript. This is useful when throttling your local bandwidth to simulate 2G or 3G speeds.

`http://www.learnhtml5book.com/chapter13/network.php`

Example 13-5 Automated Testing

How to automate testing with some Ruby and a Ruby Gem called WATIR.

`http://www.learnhtml5book.com/chapter13/watir.php`

Example 13-6 A/B Testing

How to do A/B split testing with cookies.

`http://www.learnhtml5book.com/chapter13/abtest.php`

Putting It All Together

All of the libraries created for Grandview Avenue and for this book are located at `http://www.learnhtml5book.com/test`.

Chapter 14 – Advanced Topics

This chapter introduces you to various other new HTML5-related technologies.

Example 14-1 Messaging

Cross-Domain scripting using the new messaging APIs for HTML5.

`http://www.learnhtml5book.com/chapter14/messaging.php`

Example 14-2 Server Side Events

Technology you can use to notify the web browser of an event on the server side via an event stream.

http://www.learnhtml5book.com/chapter14/serverevents.php

Example 14-3 Web Sockets

How to use web sockets with an example echo script from WebSocket.org.

http://www.learnhtml5book.com/chapter14/websocket.php

Example 14-4 Web Workers

This is a multi-threading example using JavaScript.

http://www.learnhtml5book.com/chapter14/webworker.php

Example 14-5 History Object

How to use the new history object and onHashChangei event.

http://www.learnhtml5book.com/chapter14/history.php

Putting It All Together

The Grandview Avenue app does not use these any of these technologies at this time.

Chapter 15 – Going Native

There are no examples for this chapter—just a download of the PhoneGap sample application.

http://www.learnhtml5book.com/chapter15/

Index

D, E, F

G

CPSIA information can be obtained at www.ICGtesting.com
Printed in the USA
LVOW030104270412

279370LV00004B/3/P